YOUR
magical garden

YOUR
magical garden

harness the power of the elements to create
an enchanted outdoor space

CLARE GOGERTY

CICO BOOKS
LONDON NEW YORK

Published in 2023 by CICO Books
An imprint of Ryland Peters & Small Ltd
20–21 Jockey's Fields   341 E 116th St
London   New York, NY
WC1R 4BW   10029

www.rylandpeters.com

10 9 8 7 6 5 4 3 2 1

A CIP catalog record for this book is available
from the Library of Congress and the British
Library.

ISBN: 978-1-80065-194-4

Printed in China

Senior commissioning editor: Carmel Edmonds
Editor: Slav Todorov
Designer: Geoff Borin
Illustrator: Victoria Fomina
Art director: Sally Powell
Creative director: Leslie Harrington
Production manager: Gordana Simakovic
Publishing manager: Penny Craig

Contents

SPIRIT

WATER

Releasing the magic

Sometimes, early in the morning as I walk my dog Peggy around the garden, it feels like the spirit of the earth is whispering to me. In the spring, it whispers beneath my feet as we walk beside the stream and watch rivulets of clear water course over multicolored pebbles. In the summer, it whispers in the vegetable patch as the beans lengthen and the compost heap magically softens into dark, rich mulch. In the fall, it whispers in the orchard as the apples and plums swell and drop, and the wind ruffles the leaves. And in the winter, I can hear its faint voice reminding me of another world just at the edge of my awareness.

When I first moved to this house and garden in Herefordshire, in western England, I was too busy to hear the whispering or to understand the magic beneath my feet. I couldn't shake off a lifetime of working in London—a world of deadlines and production schedules. My new life, rather than being a quiet rural idyll, was a long and exhausting to-do list much like the old one, only now lawn mowing, hedge cutting, weeding, and watering replaced meetings and deadlines.

I knew that I had arrived at a special place, but I didn't understand how to appreciate it, or stop to learn how.

Over a couple of years, though, as the garden has revealed itself, I have slowed down and tuned in. Now I notice where it feels good to sit, be still, and look at the clouds scudding over the distant hills. It felt right to eliminate straight lines where I could and introduce circles and soft edges. I tuned into the cycle of the moon and its passage across the night sky, throwing shifting, silvery shadows, and began to understand how it would affect the plants. I surrendered to the turning of the Wheel of the Year and welcomed each season with its pleasures and challenges. I planted trees with magical associations, herbs for remedies and rituals, created a wildflower fairy mound, installed a moon gate, and dowsed for energy lines.

FIRE   EARTH   AIR

Much of this has been guided by working with the four elements that are the components of all living things—Water, Fire, Earth, Air—and the fifth element, Spirit. Understanding how each of these contributes to a magical garden and how to combine them harmoniously was the key I had been looking for.

Rather than exhaust myself with planting plans and elaborate schemes, areas were left to become wild and unruly. Soon more birds arrived, pollinators zoomed in, and I could feel the garden exhale and relax. Everything, including me, was softer, quieter, calmer. I'm not a great gardener or plantswoman—anything I plant that survives feels like magic to me—but I am beginning to understand my little patch of land and how I can work with it and the elements to create something truly magical.

I still have more to do in my garden, but rather than follow an endless list of chores, I am doing one thing at a time when that time feels right. As I write this, I am creating a labyrinth in the orchard from a pile of rocks the previous owner had left behind. I intend to open the house and garden as a spiritual retreat, and the labyrinth will be somewhere guests can go for walking meditation. A firepit, representing the element Fire, already awaits them for life-affirming rituals and as a place to gather with mugs of tea, and a wood-fired hot tub (the element of Water) sits beneath the stars in a little enchanted glade tucked away under the shivering boughs of a silver birch.

The aim of this book is to encourage you to release the magic in your plot, too. By tuning into the rhythms and cycles of nature and understanding the five elements present in all things, you can awaken the spirit of your garden; whatever its size, the magic is present, waiting to be acknowledged. Even the smallest plot has the potential to become a personal sanctuary, a place of retreat, spiritual connection, and deep peace.

CHAPTER I

Where to Begin:

planning your magical garden

Getting to know your patch

Although having a garden of your own, no matter how small, is a wonderful, life-enriching thing, taking one on can feel overwhelming. There can be so many decisions to make—plants to choose, hard landscaping to consider, fences to put up. No wonder so many of us rush to the garden center and buy plants haphazardly or watch TV shows offering quick fixes.

I have learned, however, that there is another way and it's all about tuning into nature and—like nature—taking your time. Once you are in sync with the spirit of your patch and with the cycles of the seasons, everything slips into place.

A good place to start is to introduce yourself to your garden by asking a series of questions. This will help you discover what you really want it to be:

- When I come into the garden, how do I feel?

- What place do I head for?

- What can I see from the windows?

- What surrounds the garden—is it other houses, countryside, or is it something else?

- Which place do I avoid?

- Where do I like to sit?

- Does it feel too shady?

- Is there enough light or too much?

- Where do the sun and moon rise and set?

- How do I feel as I leave?

Jot down the answers—they have come from your intuition and emotional center, so are a good guide—and keep referring to them as you plan your outdoor space.

Elemental gardening

The remainder of this book is divided into five chapters, each based on one of the five elements. Acknowledging and working with the elements is a common practice in modern witchcraft and can apply equally to plants and the landscape. These elements are all around us and within us. Four of them—Earth, Air, Water, Fire—are physical, the stuff of life, and make up our bodies, the world we live in, and the universe beyond. The fifth, which goes by various names, including Spirit and quintessence (literally the fifth element in Latin), is harder to define but no less important.

The aim of working with the elements in the garden is to create a harmonious outdoor space by including all of them in equal measure. This could simply be a matter of reconfiguring your lawn into a geometrical shape (Spirit), digging a pond (Water), lighting a firepit (Fire), creating a fairy mound (Earth), and planting rustling grasses (Air). How little or how much of these elemental ingredients you include is up to you. The secret is to go for an equal amount of them all without overcomplicating matters: too much clutter and the elemental harmony is lost.

The result will be a peaceful, grounding place to sit and connect with the spirit of the earth, meditate, gather friends for a ritual, or just lie on the grass and dreamily watch the clouds and listen to the birds.

THE ELEMENTS EXPLAINED

Modern witches and pagans work with the five elements in rituals and spells, seeing them as a link to nature and the spirit world. They call on the elements to maintain stability or introduce it where things have become unsteady or out of whack. The element Spirit accompanies us on our inner journey, Water soothes and heals, Fire ignites our passions, Earth holds us and keeps us grounded, and Air refreshes and revives us.

The ancient Greeks considered the five elements as the constituents of all life, not only on this planet, but throughout the universe. Each one has its own strengths, characteristics, and correspondences (see the following chapters for explanations), but they are most powerful when they work together.

SPIRIT

WATER

FIRE

EARTH

AIR

This complementary relationship brings about an equilibrium that creates a functioning world. Keeping all five of them in balance is one way to create a harmonious and peaceful garden.

ELEMENTAL CORRESPONDENCES

Each of the four physical elements (Water, Fire, Earth, Air) is defined by certain characteristics. (Spirit is not a physical element, so doesn't have correspondences.) These include the color associated with them, symbols, and herbs, and they are used in magic work. These correspondences are also useful guides when planning a magical garden. Although they vary according to geography and tradition, most are fundamentally the same. They are explained in each relevant chapter.

THE PENTAGRAM

The elements are usually represented on the mystical symbol of the pentagram, with each one sitting at one of the five points. Spirit is at the top, with Air and Water below and Earth and Fire at the bottom (see illustration opposite). In modern witchcraft, the single point is always at the top. If a pentagram is shown upside down, with two points uppermost, it is a sign of darker magic.

This five-pointed star has recently been adopted by anyone interested in magic and the occult, but it has long been associated with mysticism. The first appearance of the symbol dates from 3500 BCE on a piece of Sumerian pottery, and it reappears in ancient Greece, Babylonia, and in European folk magic where it was used to ward off evil influences.

The magic of the pentagram is that it can be drawn in one unbroken movement comprising five straight lines. Often it is enclosed by a circle, in which case it is called a pentacle.

In my small city garden, I laid turf in the shape of a five-pointed star. While this created interesting flower beds and was a powerful place to sit or perform a ritual, the points quickly became ragged and were hard to keep sharp. An alternative would be to incorporate a pentagram into a pebble mosaic, perhaps, or to create a pentagram herb garden with different herbs in the points, each corresponding to one of the elements.

The
Wheel of the
Year and your garden

When you have a garden, you are automatically plumbed into the turning of the year. You notice and respond to the seasons and the cycles of nature. When I lived in a city, I was aware of the coldness of winter because it meant the heating was turned on and it was dark as I got on the bus home from work. The light and promise of spring were a relief after the cold months, but all it really meant was that I could put my winter coat away. Summer was welcomed because we could eat our lunch in the park, and although I liked scuffling through leaves on my way to the office, I wasn't really in tune with the melancholy beauty of the fall.

Since I've had this garden, though, the seasons guide everything I do. Not just the planning, planting, and caring for the plants, but the way I behave and what I do. City life can distance you from the cycle of the year, but having a patch of land to care for hooks you straight back in. The Wheel of the Year is the cosmic cycle of all things: birth followed by death followed by rebirth. It applies to nature and the seasons, but it also applies to our lives. It is a powerful way of seeing the world.

A year of festivals

The Wheel of the Year is a map of the seasons. Around its circumference are eight annual festivals (called sabbats in modern witchcraft) marked at equal intervals. Originally Celtic festivals, they mark the high point of each season and moments on the agricultural calendar. Two of the eight sabbats occur at solstices (the longest and the shortest days of the year) and two at equinoxes (when day and night are of equal length). These are the solar or minor sabbats, which are also known as quarter days. In the midpoints between them are the four earth or major sabbats, which are also known as cross-quarter days. (Please note: the dates given below are for the eight sabbats in the Northern Hemisphere.)

THE FOUR MAJOR SABBATS

Samhain: October 31
Plants die back and the earth slips into slumber.

Imbolc: February 2
The first stirrings of growth as the dark days recede.

Beltane: May 1
A green, fresh time of year as plants burst into life.

Lughnasadh: August 1
A time of abundance and trees heavy with fruit.

FOUR MINOR SABBATS

Winter Solstice (Yule): December 21
A few berries remain on the holly, but otherwise plants lie dormant. A still and peaceful time.

Summer Solstice (Litha): June 21
Seeds sown in spring burst into flower.

Spring/Vernal equinox (Ostara): March 21
Germination begins: seeds push up their shoots from the earth. Birds prepare nests for their eggs.

Fall equinox (Mabon): September 21
Seeds disperse on the wind. Apples grow full on the boughs and are ready for picking.

Rituals and ceremonies: a guide

The word "ritual" can be a loaded one, conjuring up visions of shadowy figures clustered around cauldrons chanting incantations. I like to think of rituals as simply symbolic acts that mark an occasion or focus attention on an intention. A ritual can be as simple as lighting a candle or writing a wish on a piece of paper and casting it into the fire.

Performing a ritual, either on your own or with others, can be a powerful way to realize your hopes and dreams. It is also a way to express gratitude for kindnesses or to celebrate what you have and what nature has provided. A ritual is especially meaningful when performed outdoors at one of the eight sabbats, or during a full or new moon. Magic is conjured up when people gather in a circle at night beneath the trees in the light of the moon. It is the sort of magic that you don't experience standing on a rug in the living room. Outdoor rituals have always been with us: from the ceremonies undertaken at ancient sites like Stonehenge, to well dressing, hanging rags above trees over sacred springs, or visiting a Buddhist shrine in a sacred place.

Any ritual I perform is guided by Druidic practice, which has a gentle, nature-loving element that I love. I belong to the Order of Bards, Druids, and Ovates, a dynamic nature spirituality that is flourishing worldwide. At its heart is a love of land, sea, sky, and, most importantly, of earth, our home.

Throughout the book, I suggest rituals and ceremonies that chime with the different elements. Overleaf are a few pointers for holding a ritual gathering, which will help you establish a way to organize your own. They are, of course, open to interpretation and adaptation. You may find yourself drawn to one of the elements more than the others depending on your needs and intent. Holding a ritual is a creative process and, as such, always evolving.

HOLDING A RITUAL: THE BASICS

This applies to rituals held with other people, although you can easily scale it down if you are practicing alone.

1 Gather everything you need Like baking a cake, you need to have your ingredients at hand in readiness. Nothing breaks the magic like hopping into the kitchen to find some salt or a candle.

2 Cast a circle This will protect anyone inside it from negative energies and keep you all safe. Place all your "ingredients" at your feet. They must stay within the circle. Trace the circle either by walking around it in a clockwise direction or marking it in the ground with a stick or an athame (a ritual knife). The size of the circle will vary according to the number of people, but one with a 10ft (3m) diameter generally works well.

3 Invite the others in Usher other participants through a "gate" in the circle cut with your hands or the athame, then close it behind them.

4 Light four candles Place the candles at each of the four cardinal points, or quarters, of the circle. As you are outdoors, the candles will need to be inside a lantern or a jam jar to prevent them blowing out or over. The four points also represent the four physical elements: north = Earth; west = Water; south = Fire; east = Air. You may decide to place something that represents each beside the candles.

5 Face east Say "Blessings to the east and all who live there."

6 Turn clockwise to face south Say "Blessings to the south and all who live there."

7 Turn clockwise to face west Say "Blessings to the west and all who live there."

8 Turn clockwise to the north Say "Blessings to the north and all who live there. The circle is cast."

9 State your purpose, such as "This is a fire ceremony to help us let go of what we don't need and replace it with what is," so that the spirit of the garden (and any garden spirits) know what you are up to and can help.

10 Work your magic.

11 Thank the spirits, the garden, and anything else you think is appropriate. Then blow out the candles.

12 Close the circle by walking around it in a counterclockwise direction.

NORTH = EARTH

WEST = WATER

EAST = AIR

SOUTH = FIRE

CHAPTER 2

Spirit

What is Spirit?

The element of Spirit is the hardest to grasp because it is not tangible. Unlike the four physical elements, Spirit is ethereal and immaterial. It has various names in different beliefs and cultures including *Akahsa*, Sanskrit for "space" or "atmosphere", "Quintessence", a name given to it by alchemists, and *Aether*, the word accorded to it by Greek philosopher Plato, meaning "pure, fresh air" or "clear sky." In the pentagram representing the five elements, Spirit is placed at the top as a presiding and unifying force. Although it has no physical presence, it is within all living things, a pulsing energy to draw on when creating your magical garden.

Unlike the other elements Spirit does not have correspondences apart from the color white, and sometimes violet and black. Symbolically it is occasionally associated with the pentacle—a pentagram surrounded by a circle—as they both hold everything together.

The magic of Spirit

In modern witchcraft, Spirit is regarded as the element that connects and balances the other four. As such, it is the conduit through which all magic passes.

GET IN TOUCH WITH THE SPIRIT OF YOUR GARDEN

Every garden has its own distinct atmosphere and character, its own spirit. Often this can be hard to discover as years, centuries even, of it being shaped by man will have hidden or disguised it. It will still be there, though, waiting to make itself known. It is what writer Lawrence Durrell calls "the invisible constant in a place" and doesn't go away. In ancient Rome, a *genius loci* was the protective spirit of the place, often shown holding a cornucopia of fruit. These spirits protected individual homes as well as entire cities. I like to think our gardens have similar guardians looking out for us in return for us taking care of them.

Discovering your garden's *genius loci* is the first thing to do when creating a magical garden. It is important to connect with the land and establish a relationship with it. You will be working together to create something wonderful, not imposing something on to it, so you have to get to know each other.

When I moved into my garden in Herefordshire in the UK, guided by the philosophy of Irish garden designer and campaigner Mary Reynolds (check out her book *The Garden Awakening*), I walked its boundaries beating a drum, pausing every so often at significant points: an old oak tree, the stream, a favorite corner. I made the drum with a shaman in Devon, southwest England, and it loves to be taken and used. (I have gone beyond worrying what the neighbors think!) Making a noise, Mary Reynolds suggests, loosens any blocked energy, and alerts the land to your arrival. It also helps to heal any areas that have been mistreated in the past.

The garden was bigger than the one I had in London and, at the start, felt overwhelming. Getting to know the space by walking around it and being attentive to its spirit made it feel more manageable. I saw my new garden as one unit rather than a lot of separate flower beds, a patch of lawn, and an orchard. I also became aware that certain areas felt different. I felt profound peace in a corner of the orchard, but there was a patch by a neighbor's fence that felt angry and out of sorts.

My slow, rhythmic walk also made me look beyond the boundary. In the distance, I could see the Malvern Hills with other smaller wooded hills rolling through the landscape toward them. I realized I wanted to reflect the surroundings in my garden and not create something discordant. I made a mental note to "shape" my garden (see page 107) by introducing heaps and mounds that echoed the faraway hills and linked the two together, so I had to plant more trees. I was grateful to the garden for revealing these things and pleased that my boundary walk made me take stock rather than rushing in haphazardly without taking its essence into account.

DISCOVERING YOUR GARDEN'S SPIRIT

Gardens are, above all, places of peace, refuge, and sanctuary. They are where we go to unkink the daily stresses, kick back, and exhale. They may not feel that way to begin with, however—certain areas could feel discordant or unhappy and need healing. The best way to tune into the spirit of your outdoor space is simply to sit in it and be still. Try this in different parts of the garden and be alert to how each one feels. Your natural intuition and sensitivity will alert you to the areas that need help and those that are happy just as they are.

One way to soothe troublesome places is to survey the garden with dowsing rods. Once I had located my unhappy spots, I took out my rods to clear away the bad energy. If you don't have rods yourself, there are local groups who will help you. (For more on this, see page 52.) Then I set to work clearing the bad energy and introducing plants that felt right for the spot.

Nature's geometry

It is tempting to adopt a free-and-easy approach when designing your magical garden; to choose wavy edges for flower beds and plant at random, thinking this is a "natural" approach. But once you look closely at nature, you see it is made up of repeated patterns. A way to understand the spirit of your patch is to work with these natural elements and incorporate them into your design. The result will be harmonious and balanced, and energy will flow fluidly through the garden, unimpeded by obstacles. Forms such as the hexagonal chambers of a honeybee hive, the perfect symmetry of a snowflake, and the spiraling pattern of sunflower seeds can all be referenced and used when you plan your garden design.

SYMBOLS AND SHAPES TO INCORPORATE INTO YOUR SANCTUARY GARDEN:

THE SPIRAL

What is it? A continuous line that winds around a central point, growing in size as it does so. Double spirals are also seen on some Irish stone carvings, as is the Celtic Triskele a triple spiral, carved into the stone passageway of Newgrange circular mound in Ireland, among other places.

Meaning and symbolism: the spiral is an ancient symbol representing eternity—there is no end to the size it can grow. It spirals inward as it expands outward—much like the human spirit which grows after a period of introspection. The spiral is associated with the Spirit element.

How to use in your garden: lay pebbles or shells in a spiral set in concrete along a path or in a seating area. Plant tall grasses in a spiral to create a 3D "whirlpool." Mow the lawn in a spiral, leaving the uncut loops to grow shaggy. Create a spiral path for walking meditation.

THE CRESCENT MOON

What is it? Also known as Luna, a half moon or sickle moon, this is the shape of the moon in the first quarter. It is used as the astrological symbol for the moon and is the alchemical symbol for the element silver.

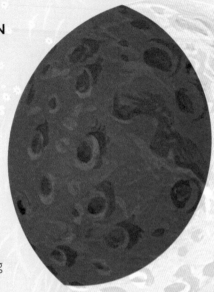

Meaning and symbolism: the crescent moon has long been regarded as a sign of fertility or virginity in many religions. The Virgin Mary is sometimes shown standing on a half moon and it was the emblem of the virgin goddess Diana/Artemis. In Hinduism, Lord Shiva can be seen wearing a crescent moon on his head, symbolizing his timelessness.

How to use in your garden: the shape of the crescent moon makes interesting flower beds. Alternatively, use it as the starting point for a pebble mosaic.

THE CROSS

What is it? Two straight lines of equal lengths crossing at right angles at their midpoints. (In Christianity the upright line is longer to represent the crucifixion.)

Meaning and symbolism: before Christianity, the cross represented balance. The vertical symbolizes spirituality and masculinity, while the horizontal is earthy and feminine. The intersection is where they come together.

How to use in your garden: use as an element of garden design. It could form the central part of a herb garden or footpaths through a vegetable bed.

VESICA PISCIS

What is it? A mathematical shape known as a "lens," formed by the interlocking of two circles of the same size.

Meaning and symbolism: In Latin, *vesica piscis* translates as "bladder of the fish"—it resembles a fish's conjoined dual air bladders. It is seen in Catholic heraldry and in Freemasonry. The cover of the Chalice Well at Glastonbury, Wiltshire, has an upright *vesica piscis* worked in metal (illustrated above). When positioned vertically, it symbolizes divine glory. When positioned horizontally, the *vesica piscis* represents the intersection of the spiritual and physical worlds.

How to use in your garden: the interlocking shapes make a good basis for a garden design or water feature.

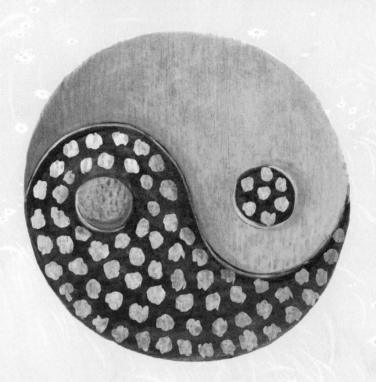

THE YIN/YANG SYMBOL

What is it? An ancient Chinese symbol of two interlocking shapes enclosed by a circle: the one on the left is light, the one on the right is black. Each shape has a circle of the opposite color inside it.

Meaning and symbolism: put simply, the yin/yang symbol represents balance and the duality of all things: the idea that all things are composed of opposing, yet complementary forces—male/female; light/dark; sun/moon. Generally speaking, yin is inward, feminine energy and yang is outward, masculine energy.

How to use in your garden: divide a circular bed with the sinuous line of the symbol. Plant either side differently—for example, turf the yang side and plant flowers in the yin side. Alternatively, create a "Zen" garden by laying gravel: light one side, dark the other, with a piece of rock at the center of each.

THE QUINCUNX

What is it? An arrangement of five objects—four at each corner of a square and one in the center, as seen on a die or playing card.

Meaning and symbolism: a quincunx is an old alchemical symbol found in the atomic structures of metals. The five points symbolize the five human senses and also represent the five elements.

How to use in your garden: setting out five new plants in the shape of a quincunx is one of my favorite ways of designing a border. It is also an excellent way to plant trees, as long as they are the correct distance apart.

THE CIRCLE:
SYMBOL OF UNITY, WHOLENESS AND PERFECTION

The previous owners of my house were keen gardeners and cleverly filled the borders with plants that flower in succession for most of the year. This was a godsend and meant I had a head start when I took over the garden. What bothered me, though, was the shape of the lawn. Or rather its lack of shape. It was large, sprawling, with edges that curled randomly around the flower beds. I hankered after geometry, a shape that made sense of the space and had symbolic meaning. I wanted a circular lawn.

The circle is a powerful shape, used in many different faiths to symbolize perfection, eternity, and wholeness. Look for it in nature and you will find countless examples, from the rings of a tree and ripples in a pond, to the sphere of a freshly podded pea. Our ancestors appreciated its power and built circular stone temples to worship those big circles in the sky: the sun and the moon.

A circle, I felt, would "center" the garden and provide a place to meditate, do yoga, and generally hang out. It would also create organically-shaped, much larger, flower beds. After a considerable amount of turf removal, soil improvement of the new beds, and sourcing of new plants, the circle was made. There have been surprising results. At times, the circular lawn draws people in and encourages them to sit in its center and be still. At other times, they walk around its edge looking outward at the plants and the fields beyond. It has been a sociable space with everyone gathering and facing each other, as well as an enclosing and safe place to be alone. It feels as though the energy of the garden is now centered and harmonious.

And as for all the turf that was removed? I used it to create a fairy mound (see page 109). My next plan is to remove the grass from the lawn entirely and replant the space with clover, or introduce a spiral path, but that's for another day.

Making a moon gate: a circular threshold

A garden becomes a more interesting place if it is divided into different areas. Stepping from one part into another feels like a mini-adventure, especially if the boundary between the two is defined. A doorway in a wall can lead to a secret garden. A hole cut into a hedge provides a glimpse and then entry into another world. A rose arch across a path welcomes you to a brand new discovery.

In my garden, I wanted to introduce a "portal" to step through from the lawn and flower borders area toward the fairy mound and the wilder, more unruly part, and I wanted it to have a symbolic meaning. A moon gate—a circular opening—was the answer. A traditional element of Chinese architecture, moon gates are usually built as part of a wall or are freestanding and constructed from stone. Their name is an obvious reference to their shape: they resemble the circular disk of the full moon.

I didn't have a convenient wall in which to install a moon gate and building one from stone was too expensive. Instead, I asked the local blacksmith to make one from steel. The height was to be slightly less than the average person, so that anyone walking through it would have to bow slightly. I love this involuntary stooping; it is like a nod to nature, an act of reverence.

Alex, the blacksmith, anchored the moon gate into the earth with a tripod of prongs welded to a circular disk on which the steel hoop was attached. Now it stands on the threshold of the strawberry patch, in front of the fairy mound, rising from the grass like the full moon ascending into the sky.

A labyrinth: an inward and outward path

The first labyrinth I encountered was on the floor of Chartres Cathedral in France on a family vacation when I was a child. Mistaking it for a maze, I walked into the tiled pattern, thinking it would take a while to find the center. Amazingly, I reached it in minutes; there was only way through. Feeling slightly cheated, I walked away and didn't give it another thought.

Years later, I rediscovered labyrinths when walking on the island of St Agnes in the Isles of Scilly. A labyrinth made of flat pebbles is laid out on the foreshore overlooking the rocks out at sea. Walking through its coils was a grounding, peaceful experience. Since then, I have understood that a labyrinth is not just an ornamental pattern that is fun to walk around, but also a tool for meditation. Its winding but purposeful path is a chance to calm the mind, focus your thoughts, and deliver you to a place of inner peace and strength.

Unlike a maze with its bewildering choice of turnings, a labyrinth has one single path that leads clockwise into the center and counter-clockwise back out again. This one-way—unicursal—route isn't direct. It switches back on itself as you near the middle. Just when you think you have arrived, you are propelled back toward the edge. Whatever twists and turns the path takes, however, you know that it will eventually take you to your destination and then safely return you to where you started. This short walk has magic in it. It can transform thinking and transcend the everyday.

Shamanic practitioner Mandy Pullen says: "Labyrinths are a way of entering inner and outer worlds while having our feet firmly attached to what we are: our land, our Earth from which we spring and to which we return. They allow us to enter a state of anchored spiritual bliss…"

Now I seek labyrinths out whenever I have a chance, especially ones made of turf or pebbles, of which there are a surprising number in the UK (I would recommend Saffron Waldon, in Essex). I like them so much that I have recreated a simplified version of the stone labyrinth at St Agnes in my garden and walk it whenever I feel the need for peace and to re-center.

CREATE YOUR OWN STONE LABYRINTH

I was fortunate that I inherited a heap of stones when I bought my house. Piled up in the orchard, they were small enough to lay on the ground and create my own labyrinth. I followed a simple, classic design, which starts with a cross and builds outward in coils (see illustration). As I write, it is almost finished! The result will be pretty rough-and-ready, but I take comfort from the fact that the one on St Agnes is similarly rudimentary.

I wanted mine to be big enough to walk through, but if you don't have the space or inclination to make one that size, you could create a much smaller one from pebbles. Rather than walk through it, you could follow the path with your eyes or trace it with a finger or a stick.

THIS WAS HOW I DID IT

I found a suitable location by dowsing (for more on this, see page 52) and asking the dowsing rods, "Where is a good place energetically to make a labyrinth?" The rods crossed dramatically at a spot beneath two apple trees. There are views of the Malvern Hills from there, and it is a peaceful spot. It felt like the earth energy was good.

I marked the outer edges of the labyrinth with grass spray paint (which washes off in the rain) to gauge its size.

The area was leveled as much as I could manage with a spade and a spirit level. Then I weeded it and dug up the turf so that only the earth remained. I had a bag of sand spare from some building work, so I spread that out to help keeps weeds at bay and the grass from returning. You could use a weed-suppressing mesh, but I'm not a big fan of these—they always escape and look messy.

I marked the coils of the labyrinth with a stick in the earth, following the design shown opposite, starting in the center and working outward.

Small stones were set into the sand along the marked lines. It took more stones than I had imagined, so, if you are going to make a labyrinth take this into account and try to estimate the number you will need first.

When the labyrinth was finished, I performed a small blessing in gratitude, then mindfully walked into its center and out again.

Mandalas: circles of life

A mandala is a kaleidoscopic, circular design, often intricate and elaborate, that crops up in various faiths as a tool for meditation and spiritual guidance. In Hindu and Buddhist traditions, for example, a mandala of interconnecting circles and squares is often embellished with symbols, figures, and animals, all focused on a central point. (*mandala* is Sanskrit for "circle.") It is a visual representation of the universe: the four directions—east, west, north, south—and the divine which resides at the center. Buddhist monks travel mentally through the mandala for hours as they meditate, until they eventually reach the divine.

Making a mandala is also a meditative process. As well as beautiful painted mandalas, Buddhist monks also create complicated mandalas made from colored sand which are destroyed when they are complete. This aligns with the Buddhist belief that nothing, however beautiful, is permanent.

We may not have the skill, patience, dexterity—or time (some take weeks)—to create a similar mandala, but our gardens can provide the materials, and the inspiration, to make something lovely and meditative of our own.

MAKE A NATURE MANDALA

Spend some time in your garden or outside in nature, collecting things that speak to you. Fallen autumn leaves, especially from trees that have significance or symbolism, are perfect, but you may be drawn to particular flowers, sticks, pine cones, lichen, small stones, seedheads, or feathers. Try to find multiples of each; the loveliness of a mandala is, in part, due to rhythm and repetition.

Sit in the garden in a place that has meaning for you and mark a circle on the ground with a piece of chalk or a stick. Mark the center of the circle, then draw eight "spokes" reaching out to the circumference at regular intervals.

Build your mandala from the center outward, starting with a single object in the middle (such as a pine cone or seed) to represent yourself. Use the "spokes" as guides to lay your natural finds in ever-increasing rings until they reach the outer edge.

Work mindfully, giving each element the respect it deserves. Pay attention to what you are making and allow yourself to be lost in the process. As you work, be aware of the sounds that surround you and the feeling of the sun or the wind on your skin. Above all, be present.

Look at what you have made and let your mind journey into the center. Acknowledge any thoughts that arise and then let them go.

Leave the mandala on the ground for others to see and to eventually blow away in the wind.

Make an outdoor altar

Although your whole garden is a sacred place, it's useful and focusing to have a designated spot—an outdoor altar—to go to. It needn't be showy—in my view, it's better if it's not—just a simple construction where you can make offerings and perform simple rituals. Start by looking around the garden for things to use. Natural materials like stones, pieces of wood, branches, leaves, mud, and feathers are best. You could also incorporate pebbles and shells you have picked up from elsewhere and that have meaning for you. Then locate a good place to build your altar. Under a tree feels right, or beside water. Dowsing may also lead to an energetic spot (see page 52).

Choose a propitious day to build your altar: equinoxes bring balance and healing; a new moon is a good time to start a project. Keep it simple: a smooth stone slab or piece of wood raised on smaller stones, or a stack of stones, works well. Consecrate your altar with the ritual described overleaf.

Now you have a place to put offerings or celebrate the different festivals throughout the year.

ALSO TRY

A stone cairn: a pile of stones laid one on top of the other and decreasing in size. Ask visitors to add a stone as an act of respect for your magical garden.

A fairy or spirit house: in the hollow of a tree to entice fairy folk form the spirit world to come over for a while.

A clootie tree: hang pieces of cloth from the branches of a sacred tree and say a prayer: make an intention or express gratitude.

AN OUTDOOR-ALTAR RITUAL

Salt has long been used in many different cultures to purify spaces, get rid of negativity, and banish spirits. Pure in its whiteness, it was thought to repel demons and evil. Today, when spilled, it is still thrown over the left shoulder by some people to blind the devil who lurks there. In modern witchcraft it is used as an agent of purification and to ward off negative influences. It represents the element Earth and is often used, along with the elements Water, Fire, and Air (incense) in magic and rituals.

It can feel positive and soothing to perform a purifying salt ritual before using your outdoor altar. Use any salt you have handy, although magical black salt (a mixture of common salt and ash) is used by some witches. Put the salt in a small bowl and place this on your altar.

Then say the following words out loud:

"I invite the spirit of the salt to work with me to protect this altar and keep it free from negativity."

Leave the bowl overnight.

The following day, say:

"This altar is pure as it can be. It is clear of all negativity."

Beating the bounds

Walking around the boundary of your land, as I did with my drum, is an ancient custom still practiced in parts of the UK and in New England, USA. Participants are mostly local bigwigs and clergymen who walk around parish boundaries, while boys hit markers with branches of willow or birch as they go. The aim is to instill the memory of the boundary on those who attend (it dates from the days when territories had yet to be mapped and GPS was not available), so they can pass it on. A version of this ceremony is an excellent way to get to know your patch of land and thank it for all it provides.

BEATING THE BOUNDS: A RITUAL WITH FRIENDS

Beltane (May 1) is a good day to do this as it's a time of dispersing the dark and welcoming the light, but that needn't restrict you: it's a lovely celebratory walk at any time.

What you do:

Before you begin, each person finds a small piece of yew (an especially magical tree with powers of protection) and blesses it with a sprinkling of water. Spring or rainwater is best, but tap water would do too.

Open the circle and call in the directions (see page 18).

Set off in procession around the perimeter of your garden. Even if the garden is tiny, this will be effective! As you walk, bless the land with the yew twig. Think of any boundaries in your life or in your mind. Are you comfortable with them or do you want to break through their restrictions? As yew is associated with the ancestors, bring them to mind and ask for their help with your intentions.

When you return to where you started, you might like to make something to remind you of what you have experienced. It would be a good time to collect flowers and ivy and make a wreath to hang on your door to keep you safe the following year. Bless whatever you make with the yew twig.

Share food and drink and what you have experienced.

Close the circle and the directions with thanks for all the blessings you have received.

CHAPTER 3

Water

The worlds of water

When I first came to look around my garden, the previous owner spent a considerable amount of time talking to me about the different sources of water I would find. He explained how to get water out of the well, when to clear the stream of watercress, how to manage rainwater collection, and how to keep the pond clear and healthy. I listened and yet I didn't really understand how vital this information was, not just to the health of the plants but to the magic of the garden.

Over the last couple of years, as I have got to know the garden, I have come to marvel at the properties of water rather than take it for granted. I diligently dig out the weeds and twigs that block the stream and enjoy seeing the water tumble and flow freely again. The well was once outside, but an extension to the house brought it indoors. I had disregarded it, walking over it (it is covered with a thick pane of glass) without a thought and even put the dog bed there. A couple of friends joined me to bless it in a simple ritual that restored it to its rightfully valued place. The pond, once depressingly full of algae, now has clear water and healthy plants. Doing these simple tasks has brought life back into the garden and filled it with a fresh and lively energy.

A garden without water is a dead, lifeless thing. It is essential to life, not just that of our gardens and ourselves, but of everything on earth. Maybe it is because of this that we are constantly drawn toward it—a survival impulse. Or maybe it's because our bodies are 70–80 percent water and we want to reunite with it somehow. The desire to be near or—even better—in, water is constantly with me, which is why I have a wood-fired hot tub (more about this on page 61). There is nothing like being immersed in water to soothe aching muscles, refresh the mind, and restore the spirit.

Like Air, Water moves easily and freely. Unlike the other elements, however, it takes many forms, from a sea fret to a tsunami to a glacier. It can take the shape of a calm, still lake, or it can thunder down from clouds in drenching, heavy raindrops.

Water has many magical associations, from water spirits to mystical springs and holy wells, rainbows above waterfalls, and sea deities. Bringing more water into the garden, and caring for what is currently there, enhances the magic that already exists.

The magic of water

Water, with its shapeshifting nature, is the element of intangible things—emotions, dreams, and the unconscious. It is also associated with psychic abilities, sensitivity, and intuition. Call on Water when doing magical work around attracting love and building relationships. If possible, find a natural source of water outdoors—a spring, stream, or pool—to carry out water-based rituals and spells. If none are within reach, collect and store rainwater.

WONDERFUL WATERY BEINGS TO CHANNEL

River and sea deities: many different mythological deities inhabit rivers all over the world, including, among many others: Oshun the patron saint of Osun River in Nigeria; Suijin the Shinto god of water in Japan; Nuliajuk, goddess of the sea's depths among the Netsilik Inuit; and Ira, guardian of the water and of the Amazon River.

Selkies: beings in Scottish mythology that change from seal to human form by shedding their skin. Similar exist in Icelandic and Faroese folklore.

Mermaids: mythical creatures with the head and upper body of a young woman and the tail of a fish. Usually depicted as beautiful with long hair and alabaster skin, they appear in the folklore, art, and mythology of many different countries. They are said to cause catastrophic consequences, such as luring mortals to their deaths, and acting as a warning of storms and dangerous seas.

Water spirits: supernatural beings who dwell in lakes, rivers, streams, and oceans worldwide. Examples include kelpies (a Celtic water horse); nixies (Germanic shapeshifters); Naids (Greek nymphs); and kappas (Japanese water sprites).

Water correspondences

The element of Water is associated with the following things—known as correspondences—which are handy to refer to when planning and planting your magical garden.

Color: blue

How to use: choose plants that reflect the colors of the sea: blues, silver, grays, and whites. In one flower bed, I planted sea holly (*Eryngium*) which is an intense blue and grows strong and tall with thistle-like flowers that last for ages. Other plants to try are *Senecio candicans* or "angel wings," which has huge, silvery-gray leaves that do indeed look like angel's wings; *Festuca glauca* ("Elijah Blue")—a low-growing grass with an intense blue color; and cornflower (*Centaurea cyanus*), an easy-to-grow annual with bright blue flowers loved by bees and other pollinators.

Sea holly

Direction: west, the place of the setting sun.

How to use: position a pool or a scrying bowl (see page 55) facing west, so that you can sit beside it and watch the sun set, infusing the water with golden light as it does so.

Time: dusk.

How to use: harness the magic of this liminal time of day to perform water spells and rituals (see page 66).

Cornflower

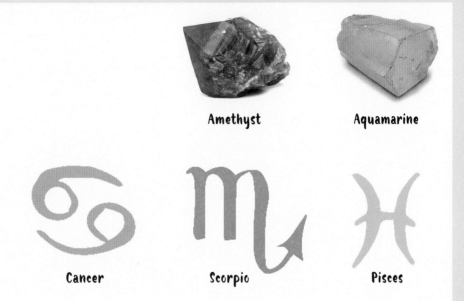

Amethyst

Aquamarine

Cancer

Scorpio

Pisces

Tool: the cup
How to use: find a small vessel that "speaks" to you. This could simply be a mug that you like or a cup associated with a person (I use a cup from a tea set that once belonged to my grandmother which has pretty blue flowers around the rim), or something you buy specially. Use the cup in water rituals or for mixing ingredients for a water-based spell.

Crystals: transparent or translucent stones, such as amethyst or aquamarine, or blue stones like blue tourmaline.
How to use: place on your outdoor altar during rituals or when spellcasting.

Zodiac signs: Cancer, Scorpio, Pisces.

The wonder of rain

"How beautiful is the rain!
After the dust and heat,
In the broad and fiery street,
In the narrow rain,
How beautiful is the rain!

How it clatters along the roofs,
Like the tramp of hoofs
How it gushes and struggles out
From the throat of the overflowing spout!"

William Wordsworth

Gardeners more than most people really appreciate rain. We are the ones who don't trust long periods of sunshine, thinking that drought must surely lurk behind. We understand that rain perks up flagging plants, soaks into the soil taking nutrients with it, fills pools, and plumps up vegetables.

My favorite place to enjoy the rain is inside the greenhouse, especially on a spring day when the garden viewed through the glass is surging with life. As I prick out seedlings the sound of it pattering on the roof is comforting; I picture it sinking into the earth and nourishing the roots of plants, and watch happily as it splashes on the surface of the pond or rushes out of the gutter into the water butt.

There is even a name for we lovers of rain: pluviophiles. A pluviophile loves rain in all its forms, from a light drizzle* to a full-on raging storm. Absence of rain causes the land to become parched and dry, but as soon as it falls, the plants spring back to life. Rain also brings puddles to splash in and rainbows to marvel at. It really is a positive force.

Different cultures throughout the ages, appreciating that rain is essential for life, have performed magic to control it. Some of these methods imitate rain to encourage its fall by, for example, sprinkling water on the ground or banging drums to simulate thunder. I prefer to listen to the weather forecast, keep an eye on the rain gauge, and grow plants that are drought-resistant and require little or no watering. (Although I'm not adverse to dancing in the rain, especially in the summer when it is longed-for and warm and splashy.)

* Although, to be fair, gray drizzly winter days are harder to love, as are interminable downpours that lead to flooding.

FIVE DROUGHT-RESISTANT PLANTS

It is increasingly important to grow plants that can resist drought as our climate changes and water conservation becomes ever more vital.

Lavender: the thin gray leaves of everyone's favorite scented shrub help it withstand dry conditions.

Salvia **"Blue Spire":** this grows vigorously in the dry part of my garden and fills the bed with spikes of violet-colored flowers in late summer and fall.

Trumpet vine (*Campsis radicans*): there is no stopping this climber which, once it gets a hold, romps up walls and fences, pushing out trumpety yellow or red flowers (depending on the species) for ages in late summer.

Common quaking grass (*Briza media*): this has pretty, heart-shaped flowers which shimmer in a breeze.

Verbena bonariensis: a tall, skinny perennial with purple flowers that has self-seeded everywhere in my garden, and very welcome it is, too.

Lavender

Common quaking grass

Rain gardens

Although storms or heavy downpours are wonderful, energizing things that feel elemental and exciting, they can, of course, cause flooding. This is especially true in urban areas where water whooshes down from drain pipes across the garden and into the drains. This isn't a problem in my garden, but in some ways I wish it was, because then I would create a rain garden.

In simple terms, a rain garden is a shallow hollow especially dug to collect rainwater, which then drains away into the soil rather than swamping everything around it. Surplus water is soaked up and stored in the soil, then taken up by flood-tolerant plants. In the process, pollutants are absorbed by the roots of the plants.

What I like about rain gardens is that not only are they beneficial to the general well-being of the garden, especially as the climate continues to change, but they also introduce a new habitat. Once the garden is up and running and the plants have become established, it will attract butterflies, bees, birds, and all manner of beneficial insects.

Making a rain garden is a fairly simple process. (The more I think about it, the more I want to make one myself.)

HERE'S HOW YOU DO IT

1 First find the right place. For a rain garden to work effectively it needs to be between two impervious surfaces—for example a patch of ground that sits between a roof and the street. Watch how the rain falls during a downpour and notice how it runs off from the gutter into the street.

2 Outline the shape of the rain garden with a piece of rope or garden hose: natural, curved forms work best, such as an oval or teardrop, for example. It is best positioned about 10ft (3m) away from the house (check there are no utility cables running beneath the soil) and should be about 42 sq ft (13 sq m) to to provide the space needed for enough plants for it to work effectively.

3 Dig a depression. This doesn't have to be very deep: about 5in (12cm) should do it. Loosen the soil a little, especially if it is heavy clay. This will help the water to drain.

4 Fill the depression with potting compost.

5 Plant with native perennials that can tolerate drought as well as downpours. Rain gardens are dry for most of the time, only holding water during and following heavy rain lasting for around 12–24 hours. Try these: yellow flag iris (*Iris pseudacorus*), purple loosestrife (*Lythrum salicaria*), meadowsweet (*Filipendula ulmaria*), and coneflower (*Echinacea purpurea*).

6 Wait for the next burst of heavy rain and watch the result.

Searching for the invisible: dowsing

I've included dowsing in this chapter because it is most often associated with finding water or metal beneath the ground. It is also, however, a way to discover any earth energy lines that run across your plot and to assess if those that do exist have been disturbed. Distortion of the earth's vibrations by underground disturbances such as drainage pipes, tunnels, or watercourses is called "geopathic stress." Some think that this can affect the health and well-being of those who live (or garden) above it. One way to discover if any such disturbance has occurred is to dowse the area.

My father was an enthusiastic dowser and was forever finding energy lines crisscrossing our garden and those of his friends. He helped one farming couple save their flock of sheep, which constantly strayed into the road to be mown down by cars. There were, he discovered, a couple of black ley lines (or a patch of geopathic stress) extending from their land to a nearby field. He—rather dramatically it must be said— staked the lines with pieces of wood and the sheep no longer wandered.

HOW TO DOWSE YOUR GARDEN

The best way to divine water or energy lines in your plot is with a pair of metal (usually copper) L-shaped rods.* You can buy these easily online at a reasonable cost.

First, think about what you want to find. I asked the rods to locate the best position to site my labyrinth, for example. You might want to find the best place for a pond, if there are energy lines crossing the garden, or something quite different. Phrase your request in terms of a question. For example: "Is there a water source beneath this lawn?"

Hold one rod in each hand with the long part parallel to the ground and facing forward. Hold the rods loosely and keep your elbows at your sides. Clear your mind and focus on your question. Keep your knees soft and slightly bent.

Repeat the question in your head and continue to do so the entire time.

Walk slowly and deliberately across the garden with the rods held loosely in your hands. Try to think about nothing except the question.

The rods will move and point in a different direction, so follow where they lead—they are guiding you to what you are looking for. When they cross over in front of your body or swing fully open, you have arrived.

* The more traditional dowsing twig—a forked branch cut from a hazel twig—is also good but harder to find. The branch dips when it locates something, a method known as "willow witching."

THE SWING OF A PENDULUM

My father always carried a brass pendulum in his pocket which he used for a variety of dowsing purposes, from identifying the sex of his first grandchild, to assessing whether a meal was nourishing or not, to what time the train I was on would arrive. Unfortunately, I no longer have his pendulum, but I do have a variety of others of my own. My favorite is teardrop-shaped and made from rose quartz, a crystal I particularly favor. I use it to ask troubling questions, or to call on the universe for guidance.

A pendulum is the simplest of devices—a piece of crystal, metal, or wood hanging from a chain—but is the key to a world of wonder. It can unlock magic, reveal energy pathways, answer troubling questions, and help you understand yourself and the world around you.

Most witches use their pendulums to clarify puzzling messages they have received, or to guide them toward a decision. The movement of the pendulum, which can either be a rotation or a swing back and forth, supplies a simple "yes" or "no" answer to any query. It is a straightforward, visual representation of the subtle energies at play around us.

Although you can use a pendulum in the garden, metal rods are more effective for large areas.

Scrying: the future in a bowl of water

The still, reflective surface of water can be a useful tool for divination, also known as scrying. Scrying is the ancient art of looking into the future by concentrating on the shiny surface of an object until visions appear. The word "scrying" derives from the Old English word *descry* which means to "make out dimly" or "to reveal" in reference to the images that appear through a thin mist.

Although crystal balls and black mirrors are the usual means of looking into the future, water-gazing, also known as hydromancy, works just as well and has a long history. Nostradamus, the French astrologer and seer, stared into a large bowl of water to receive his visions, before putting himself into a trance to interpret them.

Although you can scry indoors, it can be extra charged and more effective outdoors, especially at night during a full moon. Scryers often head to lakes or pools, but you can do it just as easily in the garden with a scrying bowl.

All you need is a large, shallow vessel filled with water. A fire bowl is good for this as long as it is clean and emptied of all debris, but a large mixing bowl also works well. Painting the inner surface of the bowl black will help, especially if you scry in daylight, but is not essential.

Find a good spot to place your scrying bowl. It needs to be away from shadows cast by trees or buildings. The only thing you want to see reflected in the bowl is the moon and your own visions! Make sure the bowl is firmly grounded and steady and fill it to the brim with water. Then you are ready to scry.

SCRYING IN THE GARDEN

Choose an auspicious day: Samhain (October 31) with all its psychic potency, for example, or the night of a full moon. If you don't have a wand, make one from a straight stick of hazel, laurel, or bay. Open a magic circle (see page 18), sit comfortably beside your bowl, and relax. Take a moment or two to settle and to tune into the sounds of the night and the feel of the wind. Touch the flat surface of the water with the wand and gaze at the ripples it makes and how they affect the reflection of the moon and the stars. Try to ignore any thoughts that arise and keep your mind clear and open. (This can be tricky but gets easier over time.) Don't stare, allowing your eyes to blink if they want to. And don't force something to happen; just be open to what you receive. After a while, a wispy mist will fill the bowl. This will thin and images will appear—they could be moving or still; just allow them to manifest. When they vanish, remember what you saw and think about what the images might mean. It could represent something that is about to occur, or it could be symbolic. It will be open to your interpretation. After ten minutes or so, stop, whether or not you have seen anything. If you did not receive an image this time, try again at the next full moon—it will come.

GAZING BALLS

Gazing balls—mirrored, stainless-steel spheres often sold in garden centers—are an alternative to scrying bowls and can be used in the same way. It is said that they were originally created to scare away evil spirits and protect the garden owner from witches, although they have also been credited with attracting fairies and bringing good luck! For our purposes, they are tools for scrying—gazing into one in a similar manner to a scrying bowl and waiting to see what appears. They also have the benefit of making attractive garden features when not used for scrying, reflecting the plants and foliage that surround them.

Water and feng shui

The pond in my garden lies just outside the kitchen window, so I can look at it as I prepare vegetables or bake a cake. To begin with, it was a source of anxiety. I worried about why there was so much algae and why there weren't any frogs and why it wasn't brimming with dragonflies. When I arrived, it was full of fish but even they had vanished. I had read countless times of the importance of water in the garden to increase biodiversity. TV presenters urged all of us to dig a pond in our gardens "if it is the only thing you do." But every time I looked at mine, my heart sank. What was I doing wrong?

Then I realized that ponds, like the rest of the garden, need to be looked after. We are, after all, custodians of our patches of land (and water), and with this comes responsibility. The pond was lifeless and full of algae because it had become congested with plants. The pump powering the fountain had broken, so the water wasn't oxygenated. The fish had vanished because the heron had taken them. I had been topping up the pond with tap water when all the time I could have used fresh, life-giving water from my own well.

To tackle all of this, alongside all the usual gardening books and online links, I consulted a book I had on feng shui that had been lying on my bookshelf for years. The principles of feng shui (see overleaf) chimed with my approach to elemental gardening, and made a lot of sense.

FENG SHUI GUIDANCE ON WATER IN THE GARDEN

- Locate any pond or water feature in the north, east, or southeast corners of the garden to bring prosperity and wealth.

- Water should flow toward the house, perhaps the main entrance, or a large window to allow chi to enter the home. It should never flow away from the house.

- Water flow in fountains should be moderate and consistent. You don't want a raging torrent or a measly trickle. Somewhere between the two is just right.

- Remove dead plants and fallen leaves as they can restrict the flow of chi. This also makes good horticultural sense.

- Water must be of good quality and topped up regularly to keep the pond fresh and free of algae.

After some time and application, the pond has come back to life.* The view from the kitchen window is now a delight, not a worry. The fountain gushes and sparkles in the sunlight, bringing life, sound, and oxygen. The water is clear and algae-free and the plants around the edge, cleared of dead leaves and debris, are thriving. And, best of all, dragonflies and newts have arrived. The pond's magic has been restored.

* Although not the fish, unfortunately—the only way to keep them safe from the heron is to cover the pond, which I am reluctant to do.

FENG SHUI IN A SNAPSHOT

Feng shui is the ancient Chinese art of placement. Broadly speaking, it is about harnessing natural energy flow, known as chi, to create a balanced life that is in harmony with the environment. In the garden, this is achieved by the careful placing of plants and structures to enable chi to flow. When it flows without obstruction, health, prosperity, and abundance follow.

Translated literally *feng shui* means "wind-water" and comes from an old Chinese poem describing ideal living conditions:

- **The winds are mild**
- **The sun is bright**
- **The water is clear**
- **The trees are lush**

It is a useful and powerful way of planning a garden. Water elements, especially those that make a pleasing sound, are recommended—water is associated with the flow of chi—as are well-placed stones with sculptural shapes. Harmonic sound and swaying grasses and bamboo are also important (see page 124 for guidance on using wind chimes), as is the introduction of light and air by pruning. Meandering paths are introduced to give the illusion of flowing space and movement.

Fundamentally, feng shui is all about returning to the state of balance in nature's default setting. Facilitating this is an important part of creating a sacred garden, and feng shui is one way to do it.

FIVE WATER-LOVING MARGINAL PLANTS:

Miniature water lily (*Nymphaea "Pygmaea Helvola"*): the pale-yellow flowers with orange stamens are just lovely. A good size for a small pond, larger varieties will take over.

Arum lily (*Zantedeschia aethiopica*): the beautiful white blooms against glossy green foliage look spectacular and gracious.

Marsh marigold (*Caltha palustris*): an easy-to-grow marginal plant with cheery, buttery-yellow flowers in spring.

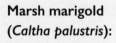

Water soldier (*Statiotes aloides*): I have this in my pond as it makes a nice contrast to the flat leaves of the water lily. Its spiky leaves surface from the depths in spring, then sink back down again in winter.

Corkscrew rush (*Juncus effusus f. spiralis*): this has twisty, spiraling stems that look good in a small or contemporary pond where they can be seen and admired.

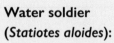

Water dipping

The only reservation I had about moving to rural Herefordshire was how far it was from the sea—as far as it is possible to get in the UK. There are also no pools nearby to swim outdoors; my house in London was near a large and lovely lido. My dream one day—watch this space!—is to create a natural pool in the paddock beside the orchard. I picture a long lane pool whose edges brim with plants and on which ducks paddle at eye level as I swim among them. Then I could have a dip every morning without leaving the boundaries of the garden. How lovely would that be!

In the meantime, I have installed a wood-fired hot tub which sits in a coppice of hazel trees tucked away from the rest of the garden behind a little wooden fence. I love making my way down there with friends at dusk, towels over our arms, to be greeted by the smell of wood smoke and the sight of steam rising temptingly from the tub. I can lose all sense of time and place in that tub, especially when the stars come out, the birds fly back to their roosts, the trees rustle overhead, and nocturnal creatures scurry about in the undergrowth.

Conversations start softly as secrets are shared, then peter out as we all enjoy the simplicity of being in water, heated by the crackling fire, in each other's company, outdoors. Just being there is an escape from the humdrum everyday to a more enchanted world. At other times, I go there alone, to meditate and be still. There is something about sitting in a tub of hot water that is profoundly relaxing.

THE BENEFITS OF AN OUTDOOR SOAK

A survey by Coventry University in the UK suggested that a prolonged soaking in a hot tub has similar benefits to aerobic exercise. The evidence suggested that it can help reduce the risk of cardiovascular disease. Sitting up to your shoulders in a hot tub heated to approximately 104°F (40°C) for one hour can raise core temperature and improve blood flow, which can lower blood pressure, control blood sugar levels and reduce inflammation. It can also help you sleep and boost energy levels. Plus, it forces you to slow down and do nothing but listen to the wind and the birds: reason enough in my book to do it as often as possible.

A note of caution: be wary of any dizziness or becoming dehydrated. Take water to drink and carefully and slowly step out if you feel light-headed.

The simple business of immersion in water, whether it's the whole body in a tub, the toes in a stream, or the hands and face in a holy well, feels sacred. I always approach it reverentially and with care, mindful of its wonder and mystery. Bathing and ritual washing with water are holy activities in many faiths and religions, including Christianity, Hinduism, Islam, and Judaism, and have been since ancient times. All recognize the importance of water, not just to sustain life but also to cleanse and to purify. There are also very many water deities across all faiths, often representing the spirit of a river or a holy well, or the ocean itself, as well as mythical creatures, including sirens, water nymphs, and mermaids. Water, it seems, inspires wonder in all of us.

"Live in the sunshine, swim the sea, drink the wild air."

Ralph Waldo Emerson

ALTERNATIVE WAYS TO GET INTO WATER IN THE GARDEN

- **Paddle**. You don't need a stream running through the garden or a huge pond: a child's paddle pool or a large basin will do. Fill it with water: if possible, use rainwater; installing a water butt to collect it from a gutter is well worth the effort (and has the bonus of being a water source for plants). Take off your shoes and socks, put your feet in the pool, and relish the feeling of the cold water, feeling grateful for its healing, cleansing, purifying, and nourishing qualities as you do so. The water will be cold, but it will be invigorating!

- **Get out the garden hose**. Whenever my friend Kate comes to stay, she rigs up an outdoor shower by dangling the garden hose from a silver birch bough. On hot summer days when we have been out in the sun for too long, nothing is as refreshing as standing, gasping, under a fountain of cold water, noticing how the water sparkles in the sunlight. (It is also fun to turn the garden hose on any passing children and make them squeal.)

- **Wash your face outdoors**. Doing something outside that normally takes place inside the house always shakes things up and makes the day feel more exciting. This is lovely to do on a spring or summer morning when the sun has just risen. Fill a bowl with water, either rainwater or warm water from the tap for a treat! Take the bowl outside with some soap (or whatever you use to wash) and a towel and carefully wash your face. Do this slowly and, as you do so, notice how the water feels on your skin and how your face feels afterward. It is like giving yourself a blessing and sets you up for the day.

- **Make a plunge pool**. This may sound fancy but all you need is a vessel big enough to cover you to shoulder level. If you live in the country, auctions are good places to find old containers used for agricultural purposes that, so long as they don't leak, make good plunge pools. The water won't be heated, but it will be exhilarating. Fill the pool almost to the brim, get in (a stool or small ladder will help you with this), and bob about up to your neck for as long as it is (reasonably) comfortable. It is—honestly—worth it.

Dew: a sparkling magic carpet

There is something magical and otherworldly about dew. It appears in the garden overnight jeweling blades of grass and spider's webs, and leaves a twinkling coating of minute droplets. And then, as the day warms up, it vanishes, evaporated by the heat of the sun. On summer mornings when I go to feed the chickens, I like to walk barefoot across the lawn to the orchard where the hen house is. The cold, wet dew on the short grass is lovely and refreshing on the soles of my feet. (An old tradition says that walking barefoot in dew prevents corns and bunions—so far, for me, so good!)

There are many other customs and traditions associated with bathing in dew, many taking place on auspicious days: especially Beltane (May 1) with all its fresh spring promise, and the Summer Solstice (June 21) when the sun is at its most powerful. Dew collected from the leaves of hawthorn and oak was considered especially potent. In Icelandic folkloric tradition, dew bathing took place on the eve of Jonsmessa (Midsummer Night) June 21, the longest day of the year, when the sun never sets.

"The fair maid who the first of May
Goes to the field at the break of day
And washes in dew from the hawthorn tree
Will ever after handsome be."

[Old nursery rhyme]

Young Scottish and Irish women washed their faces in dew, hoping it would preserve their youthful beauty and increase their chances of childbirth. (Men, on the other hand, were said to wash their hands in it to increase their abilities to open knots and locks.) Bathing naked in dew was said to keep the skin soft, ease sunburn, and prevent wrinkles. (See page 64 for a modern bathing ritual.) To continue to harness the power of dew throughout the year, many folk collected it at Beltane and bottled it. This is a handy and enjoyable thing to do and means you will have a store of dew handy to anoint magical tools and to use in spells.

HOW TO COLLECT DEW

Gather everything you will need: some strips of cloth, a container with a lid, and a bag or basket to carry them in.

Check the time of the sunrise the night before and set the alarm for that time.

Get up and go out into the garden. Look for the dew. Even the smallest garden should have some on the lawn or on the leaves of shrubs or trees.

Take a rag and either wipe dew-laden leaves or drag it through the grass. In old Irish traditions, people would whack pieces of linen through long grass and hedgerows.

Wring out the rag, once it is thoroughly wet, into the container.

Continue with the other strips of rag until you have collected enough to fill a bottle. Return home and filter the dew to remove any bits of vegetation, insects, and so on.

Pour it into a bottle (a funnel will help with this), and put in the stopper.

The dew is ready to use in future magical work. It is not suitable for drinking, though, so don't be tempted!

DEW PONDS

If you go walking on the chalky uplands in parts of England (West Sussex especially), you may come across wide, saucer-shaped indentations filled with water. These are dew ponds, which were created in the 18th and 19th centuries by farmers to provide water for livestock in areas where none occurred naturally. Also known as cloud or fog ponds, the water comes from moisture that condenses upon its cool surface at night (the definition of dew). Although man-made, they are also mysterious and enchanting, and reflect the sky above and the passing clouds.

It is possible to make a dew pond in your garden, and I have given this some thought as it would be handy to provide an extra water source for my sheep. Ideally, though, the garden needs to be in a high place, and the dew pond should be about 33 sq ft (10 sq m). It must be lined with an insulating geo-textile blanket to ensure the water remains colder than the earth, as well as a tough waterproof membrane. Once that is all sorted, all you do is wait for the dew to collect.

Water spells and rituals

BATHE IN THE DEW

This is best performed at Beltane (May 1), as the sun rises, and when the dew is still fresh. The dew is said to be especially refreshing at this time of year and will cleanse skin and generally beautify the parts of you with which it comes into contact.

- Set the alarm for sun rise. Wake up and immediately head for the garden where the dew is heaviest.

- Take off your shoes and stand in the dew.

- Notice how the dew feels—its temperature, how wet it is—and how your feet feel in response.

- Ground yourself by standing with your legs a hip-width apart, keeping the back of your neck long and your arms hanging loosely by your side.

- Visualize a beam of light coursing through your body, entering all its nooks and crannies before flowing into the earth.

- Drop into a kneeling position and lay your hands flat on the ground in front of you.

- Scoop up as much dew in your hands as you can.

- Wash your face with the dew, enjoying the feeling of the clean, fresh, cold water on your skin. (You could also remove all your clothes and roll around in the dew for a complete, wrap-around effect.)

- Let the dew dry naturally.

- Stand up and visualize the beam of light leaving your body.

MAKE MOON WATER

During a night when the moon is full, carry out this simple ritual to charge water with lunar energy. The water can be used in spells, to power up crystals or magic tools, or to bless something of meaning or someone close to you. You could also add a splash to your bath or to wash your hair (said to improve mental clarity), or spritz around the house to protect it.

Fill a glass or jar with rainwater or water, preferably collected from a spring or holy well, but filtered tap water will do. Avoid using plastic containers: a glass jam jar works perfectly well.

Sprinkle sea salt and drop a clear quartz crystal into the water for extra whizz.

Hold the glass or jar close to your heart and visualize the water filling with light and love.

Place the jar in the beam of the full moon.

Surround the jar with talismans, herbs, and crystals that chime with a particular intention or wish.

Leave the jar in the light of the full moon to fully charge until morning. Then collect the jar and store it somewhere dark and cool until you want to use the moon water.

ELEMENTAL FLASH RITUAL: DANCE IN THE RAIN

Shifting your mindset to love the feeling of rain falling on your head and face—rather than shrinking inside a jacket and pulling up a hood—is a liberating thing. It's certainly worth a try, especially on a summer's day when the garden is desperate for a shower and the rain is warm and heavy. Dance barefoot on the lawn and allow yourself to be thoroughly drenched. Any old dance moves will do; they become a little more crazy when you are getting soaked. The rain won't hurt you and, anyway, as a Buddhist friend of mine says: "When you're wet, you're wet." Then you can run inside, get dry, and feel like a truly elemental being.

CHAPTER 4

Fire

Harnessing the power of fire

Fire is intense, urgent, and unpredictable. It can destroy everything in its path, yet it brings light to darkness and warmth to outstretched hands, and provides a place to cook. Unlike the other elements, fire can't be touched, yet it roots us to the earth, and to ourselves, in a fundamental way.

Some of my most magical and memorable moments have occurred outside, at night, around a fire with friends. Anyone who has gathered around a bonfire and watched the flames flicker and dance will appreciate its magic. Watching them rise and spark, then dwindle, is mesmerizing, as is the flickering light they create and the intimate feeling a fire creates. Creating a simple fire ritual boosts the experience further; it honors this most capricious element and harnesses its power.

Every garden should have somewhere to light a fire and appreciate its elemental pull. My garden has two places where the crackle of wood and the smell of wood smoke can be found: the firepit and the hot tub (see page 61). Both are in the orchard, which is a little way from the house and is the wildest part of the garden. At night, or dusk, walking from the cozy domesticity of the house, past the vegetable beds, and through the field gate to the orchard feels like a journey into another world. This is heightened, of course, if a full moon has risen into a star-sprinkled sky, and the destination is an open fire with its beckoning flames. (It is also lovely to return to the house with a warm nose, smelling of wood smoke and wrapped in blankets.)

As the seasons change and the Wheel of the Year turns, fire can be celebrated in different ways. At Samhain (October 31), the start of the witch's year, fires are lit to banish the darkness and to remember the ancestors. (In the UK, this festival has morphed into Guy Fawkes Day, or bonfire night.) It's a time to set intentions for the year ahead and to remember friends and family who are no longer with us. It is also a time to watch steam rise from a mug of hot chocolate as the limber flames twist and the embers crackle.

Fire is at the heart of Beltane (May 1). Beltane means "bright fire," and bonfires were traditionally lit to increase the fertility of crops and livestock. People would dance *deosil* (clockwise) around the fire for good luck and protection against illness, and cattle were encouraged to leap over the embers to keep them in good health. Beltane is a good time to practice fire rituals (see page 85) either with others or alone, especially if you need to balance the male and female aspects of your life or find a partner.

Sitting outdoors around a fire at the time of the Summer Solstice with friends can be a moment of enchantment. Traditionally, the solstice was celebrated with fire to honor the sun and to boost its strength. Bonfires were lit on high ground, burning wheels rolled down hills, and lovers jumped over the flames to seal their union. A Summer Solstice bonfire remains a joyful, celebratory thing. As the light in the sky dims, the fire seems to burn more fiercely and brightly. Everyone gathers closer, poking it with sticks, adding logs, toasting marshmallows, sharing stories. The ever-shifting flames rise and subside, and noses fill with the fragrant smell of wood smoke. As the stars come out and the temperature drops, sweaters are pulled on and, if magic is in the air, talk turns to a fire ritual.

THE MAGIC OF FIRE

Fire, with all its fierce yet life-enhancing power, stands for energy, passion, transformation, and healing. Connecting with fire is a good way to fuel yourself with courage and strength when you need to deal with big, challenging things. It is also purifying and protective, driving back the darkness and keeping away potential harm. A fire ceremony outdoors allows you to connect deeply to the earth, the natural world, and the stars. It also, by its transformational power, enables you to change direction or patterns of behavior.

Fire correspondences

The element of Fire is associated with the following things—known as correspondences—which can be incorporated when you are planning and planting your magical garden.

Colors: red and orange, the colors of flames.

How to use: plant red hot pokers (*Kniphofia*) for their bright fiery spears—they even look like flames. Grow the Mexican sunflower *Tithonia rotundifolia* "Torch" from seed: it's an annual whose gorgeous orange flowers bring much cheer to a late-summer garden. Similarly, the bright orange *Cosmos sulphureus* is the color of the sunset on a summer day.

Red hot poker

Direction: South.

How to use: If you are lucky enough to have a south-facing garden, you will know how lovely it is to bask in the sun. This, then, is the place to put a lounger and enjoy the blessings, warmth, and light the sun brings. It is also an ideal place to grow sun-loving plants like succulents and Mediterranean herbs such as lavender and rosemary. Or plant a fig. Just remember to water when the sun gets too hot.

Time: noon.

How to use: this is an auspicious time to cast a fire-based spell, to attract more love into your life, perhaps, or to strengthen your courage. Cast the spell in the southern part of the garden.

Mexican sunflower

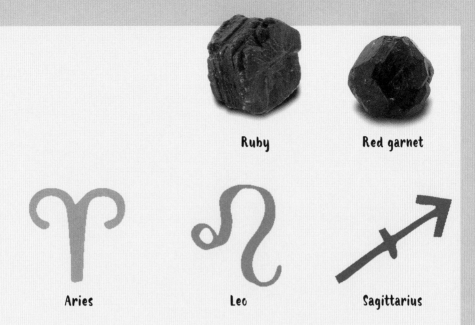

Ruby

Red garnet

Aries

Leo

Sagittarius

Crystals: fire opal, ruby, garnet.

How to use: place on your outdoor altar before casting a circle (see page 18) or starting a ritual. Remember to collect the crystals when you have finished.

Magical tools: athame, wand.

How to use: make sure your athame or wand is the center of any fire-based rituals you hold outdoors.

Zodiac signs: Aries, Leo, Sagittarius.

Cosmos sulphureus

ON FIRE: SIX FABULOUS FIERY BEINGS TO CHANNEL

The salamander: a spotty, lizard-like amphibian once thought to live in fire and not be affected by it (untrue!). In mythology, it burst into flames. Salamanders can also regenerate limbs.

The phoenix: a bird from Greek mythology that lived for centuries in the desert before burning itself on a funeral pyre, then rose from the ashes with renewed youth to live again.

Brigid: Irish goddess (also known as Bride or Brighid) associated with wisdom, poetry, blacksmithing, and healing. Her feast day is February 1 (Imbolc on the Wheel of the Year), when she was celebrated with bonfires, lit to protect cattle and provide a fruitful harvest.

Prometheus: the Greek god of fire, which he stole from the gods to give to man.

Loki: the shapeshifting Norse god of chaos and mischief, who is also associated with fire.

Spider Grandmother: in Native American mythology she stole fire from the sun and hid it in a clay pot to give to the people, so they could see in the darkness.

The phoenix

CANDLE MAGIC

If you have ever attended a torchlight procession, especially one at Samhain (October 31) or Beltane (May 1), you will understand the magic, drama—and perils—of carrying fire. When the Wheel of the Year is at its darkest point at midwinter, a bonfire brings people together to stand around its light and warmth, to exchange stories, to dance and make intentions.

At any time of year, however, fire works best at night. If you don't have a firepit or fire bowl and aren't heading to a public bonfire or torchlight procession, candles will do the job just as well. Include them in your outdoor rituals or spells, making sure they are secured safely or carried in a lantern. Even the activity of carrying a lantern through the garden feels magical, as it opens up the darkness and throws crazy shadows around you.

In spellcasting, different colored candles have different properties: green or pink for love, yellow for wealth, red for strength, blue for luck, mauve for wisdom, brown for stability. A simple spell to draw something toward you is to write what it is from the top of the candle to the bottom and let it burn out. A candle is also a powerful meditation tool: gazing softly into its flame (called *trataka* in yogic practice) can help the mind to focus.

Cauldrons: a magical pot

The familiar black, pot-bellied pot with its three legs has come to symbolize witchcraft. Much of this is due to its representation in art and culture: the three witches in *Macbeth*, for instance, hovered over a bubbling cauldron as they brewed up their particularly nasty potion.

I like to see the cauldron as a much friendlier vessel: a useful pot in which to burn incense (place incense on charcoal disks in the base of the pot), or to use for a fire ritual when lighting a fire is too much trouble.* It also works wonderfully hooked over the smoldering embers of a fire to use as a simple cooking pot or to boil water for tea.

In my garden, I have created a firepit (see page 78) in the orchard with a simple wooden structure above it from which to hang my cauldron. On clear, twinkling fall nights around the full moon, it feels especially magical out there, stirring something in the pot above glowing logs. It is a wonderful way to connect with the element of Fire, watch the heat pulsing in the embers, and smell the wonderful fragrance of wood smoke.

BUYING A CAULDRON

I was lucky to inherit a cauldron with the house when I bought it. It is a stout cast-iron pot with three sturdy legs and a hooped handle, which—going by the amount of dirt inside it—the previous owner used for houseplants. Finding it in the garage was a sign that this house has something magical about it. The cauldron has been liberated from pot plant duties and I now put it to use for rituals, mixing herbal concoctions, and stirring incense ingredients.

Take care when buying your cauldron: many of those on the internet are flimsy and not fit for magic work. Find a cast-iron one if possible and make sure to know its measurements: some of those advertised are more decorative ornaments than functioning tools.

* This is a good way to hold a fire ritual safely indoors alone. A stout cauldron can contain a small fire, as long as you watch it closely. Build a mini fire in the cauldron with dry leaves or shredded paper with a thin stick placed on top. Throw in herbs that are appropriate for the time of year of the ritual you are performing. Have a bucket of water ready just in case.

COOKING IN A CAULDRON

Your three-legged pot needn't be restricted to magical purpose. It can also be used to cook simple meals such as soups and stews, or to boil water for tea or herbal infusions. Make sure to clean it thoroughly afterward or have a separate cooking cauldron. You don't want future magic contaminated. A meal cooked above an open fire is the perfect post-fire ritual feast.

You could place the cauldron directly on the fire, but I prefer to hang it from a simple structure or a tripod above the heat. Use the lid, if it has one, to speed up the cooking.

CAULDRONS IN MYTHS AND FOLKLORE

The cauldron is shrouded in fabulous tales of witchcraft, sorcery, and alchemy stretching back for centuries.* In Irish folklore, a cauldron is where the mischievous leprechauns keep their treasure. It was also thought that a magic cauldron never ran out of food at a feast. In Welsh mythology, it is associated with the enchantress Cerridwen, the goddess of rebirth and transformation, whose cauldron was the source of poetic inspiration, known as *Awen*. In the Celtic legends of the *Mabinogion*, the Cauldron of Rebirth (the *Pair Dadeni*) is a magical pot in which one can revive the dead. Another Celtic god, Cernunnos, the horned god, was torn apart and boiled in a cauldron to be born again. In Norse mythology, the god Odin drank magic blood from a cauldron of wisdom to gain divine power. It was also an important tool for alchemists in their attempts to turn base metal into gold.

In modern witchcraft, the cauldron with its curvaceous shape and enclosing form has come to symbolize the goddess and the womb. It also represents the mysteries of creativity, femininity, and the wisdom of Mother Earth.

*The earliest cauldron dates back to the late Bronze Age: it has a 13–15 gallon (60–70 liter) capacity, so chances are that it was used for cooking.

Fire in the garden

A NOTE ON FIRE SAFETY

While I love the ferocious and unpredictable nature of fire, I also appreciate that it can be a dangerous thing. When lighting a fire, make sure you do so well away from the house and/or any hanging branches. Make sure to have a bucket of water or sand handy (or a fire extinguisher) to extinguish any unwanted flames, and keep children and animals at a safe distance at all times. It's a good idea if one person is designated as "fire warden" to monitor the flames and their safety.

FIREPITS

A bonfire with crackling logs and leaping flames is a beautiful, elemental thing. It can, however, be too fierce and unruly for most gardens and is best restricted to public events where it can be controlled. A firepit, however, is an excellent alternative, which suits domestic spaces and smaller gatherings.

I hesitated before digging my firepit, wondering if I would ever actually use it. I am glad I did: it is just the right size to get a fire going quickly and there is room around it for a few like-minded folk to gather. Perfect for a spot of intention setting, dreamy flame watching, roasting chestnuts, and toasting cold hands. I also like to scatter herbs and incense on the embers for seasonal aromas.

HOW I MADE MY FIREPIT

I found the right place. My firepit is in the wild part of the garden, but fairly near the house for easy access. I dowsed the land first with divining rods (see page 52), asking the question "Where is the best place to connect with the element of Fire?" The rods indicated the perfect spot. Fortunately, it was also a safe place: several feet away from trees, bushes, and the house, and on a flattish piece of ground. The nearby stream is also handy in case emergency dousing is needed! Although firepits generally contain the fire, the burning wood can still send sparks flying dangerously into the air. It is also worth checking that no utility cables or pipes run beneath the ground.

Then I marked the circumference of the firepit with a temporary spray marker. The size/shape will depend on how big your pit will be and how you construct it. I used a circular firepit ring liner. This sits inside a circular hole and contains the fire.

I removed the turf within the marked outline with a spade (mine is circular but you could make a square one if you fancied it).

Then I dug the hole. This was the most labor-intensive part, but fortunately it had just rained, so the earth was still soft and easy to remove. If you use a similar steel ring, you could skip the digging and simply place it on the ground, removing the grass inside it first. Made of steel, the ring liner came in four pieces which bolted together easily. It is also portable, so you could pack it up and take it camping.

Finally, I built the surround. This is not essential but there was a pile of stones and rocks left in the orchard, so I used those. I laid them around the edge of the firepit ring liner in a couple of layers to finish it off.

Then I lit the fire.

MAKING A FIREPIT

1 Dig a circular hole to the same dimensions as the steel firepit ring liner so it will fit snugly inside.

2 Insert the steel ring liner into the hole, then surround it with stones to hide the edge.

3 Add another layer of stones to make a more substantial structure, although this is optional.

THE BEST WAY TO LIGHT A FIRE

Learning to light a fire is one of the modern witch's most useful skills. I love lighting fires—indoors, nothing says "cozy" like a real fire, and outdoors little is quite so magical. Getting a good blaze going feels like a real accomplishment. Creating a fire from nothing but kindling and pieces of wood is a kind of magic in itself. Once lit, the fire brings light, warmth, and drama into the garden, and creates a focal point for gatherings. Although fire lighting can stump some would-be fire-starters, get a few basics right and you won't go far wrong.

Choose your wood carefully. This is important: you want a long, steady burn rather than a flash in the pan. Hardwoods like oak, ash, and beech are best and generate less smoke. Soft woods like pine are easier to get going, but burn faster. Make sure the wood is "seasoned," i.e., dry. You can usually tell by its weight; dry wood is much lighter. If you source your own wood from trees (avoid any painted or treated wood as it may give off harmful chemicals), or logs found in woodland (check local rules), you will have to store it until it dries out. Wood bought from log suppliers and grocery stores, for example, is good to go.

Build your fire. In the firepit, make a pile of dry twigs, pine cones, and leaves or crumpled-up paper. Then cover with a "teepee" of larger pieces of wood. Fires need oxygen to ignite, so don't pack the wood too tightly.

Light your fire. Using a match, light the dry bits of tinder. (Avoid paraffin firelighters or lighter fuel as they can be uncontrollable.) You may need to blow gently to get the flames going. Feed the fire with more tinder as it gets established, and add larger pieces of wood and logs as it grows.

Let the fire settle. After the initial blaze, let the fire calm down until it has reduced a little and has a few red-hot embers. Keep an eye on it, adding more wood when necessary.

FIRE BOWLS

For a quick and easy way to get a mystical blaze going in the garden, try a fire bowl. These ready-made metal dishes (often sold as "firepits" confusingly) come with legs or stands and are widely available from home- and garden stores in a variety of sizes and at a range of prices. They make a useful and attractive addition to the garden and are very handy for fire rituals and gatherings. Small fires can be lit in them in the same way as a firepit.

Working with the sun

The sun is the element of Fire embodied. An enormous ball of fire, around which the earth revolves, it is the heart of our existence, providing us with light and warmth. Without it, we could not survive. Our ancestors knew this as well as we do, erecting huge solar monuments like Stonehenge in the UK to monitor its movements and worship its power (see page 83).

Modern witchcraft is often moon- rather than sun-orientated, and it's easy to see why. The moon appears to be more magical, growing fuller throughout the month, its 13 full moons synchronizing with women's cycles and controlling the tides. Rising magnificently at night and casting a silvery light, it wins hands-down on the magical ratings.

It would be a mistake to ignore the sun, however, and it is important to respond to it in your magical garden. This could be as simple as growing plants that correspond with the element of Fire (see page 72), or placing a deckchair in a sunny sheltered spot to lie in its warmth, and absorb its life-giving energy. (Sunbathing is as magical as moon bathing in my book!) Or you could add extra elements like a sundial, create a mini stone circle, or install a carefully positioned boulder (see page 83).

SUNDIALS: READING THE SHADOWS

In later life, my father became fascinated with sundials. Not just learning about them and scouring the country looking for examples, but making them, too. His specialty was the armillary sphere—interconnected metal rings representing astronomically important features—but he also made window dials, wall dials, and four-sided dials. As a result, our garden and neighborhood—he made and donated dials to local churches—became peppered with sundials.

Since then, I have always had a fondness for sundials and keep an eye out for them when visiting gardens or looking around graveyards and churches. I love the way the shadow from the sun moves around the dial telling the time as the sun travels across the sky. It is a direct line of communication with solar energy. It is also a reminder of the passing of time and the impermanence of all things. Many sundials are inscribed with sobering mottos like *tempus fugit* (Latin for "time flies"), or *umbra sicut hominis vita* ("a person's life is like a shadow").

I learned from my dad that most sundials are positioned badly or have incorrectly aligned gnomons (the pointy bit that casts a shadow). This means that the shadow falls on the wrong place and you cannot read the time accurately, if at all. If you choose to install a sundial, make sure to set it up properly. Otherwise, it's merely decorative and rather pointless, especially in your magical garden where things are placed with consideration and purpose.

WHERE TO PUT A SUNDIAL

Place a horizontal sundial in a sunny, preferably south-facing, part of the garden, ensuring it is oriented toward true north (this is not magnetic north as found on a compass). The website solar-noon.com will tell you the exact time of solar noon wherever you are. When you know this, rotate your dial until the shadow falls on the number 12. Then it will point to true north, and you are all set.

Make the sundial the centerpiece of a daytime fire ritual, or simply use it to read the time and marvel at its connection with the sun and the universe beyond.

The magic of stones

Wherever I travel throughout the UK, I keep an Ordnance Survey map handy in the glove compartment to look out for ancient megaliths, stone circles, burial chambers, and other prehistoric sites. They are always worth a diversion along a minor road, or a tramp across a field. Our ancestors were more connected with the land than we are by virtue of their way of life: their survival depended on it. They were also more aware of the night sky and the movement of the sun and moon. There were probably practical considerations for erecting these monuments, but often it feels as if they erected them for a spiritual purpose. Stones, for example, were frequently hauled great distances to stand at specific spots, often on headlands or hilltops with breath-stealing views.

Many stone circles were aligned with different positions of the sun. Stonehenge's Trilithon faces the sunset of the Winter Solstice and, if you stand in the center of the circle at midsummer, the sun rises to the left of its Heel Stone. Entering a stone circle (my favorite is the Rollright Stones in Oxfordshire) and sitting beside one of the huge megaliths can be a profoundly peaceful experience.

I love big stones and boulders. They are strong, silent, ancient, and a constant presence. They hold memories of the landscape within their massive bulk. They feel indestructible. Some pagans believe that they house the spirits of living creatures. My dream is to introduce one into my garden but, alongside practical considerations—weight mostly—I would hesitate to remove one from its current location.

One day I will create my own mini stone circle—see overleaf for how I will do it.

MAKING A MINI STONE CIRCLE

Sketch a diagram of your stone circle using a favorite one as a template. Remember to include an entrance point: a couple of slightly larger stones that will act as a portal. How and where you enter a circle is important to get right. You may also want to include a stone at the center, or a mini firepit to light a candle.

Think about alignments with the sun: where does the sun rise at the solstices? Choose one alignment and place your stones so that the sun's rays will strike a particular one at a certain time.

Find your stones. Local is best as this will connect you to the geology of the land around you. My local stone is a type of granite: you can see it used in walls and houses throughout the village. Otherwise, look in builders' yards, making sure the stones come from a sustainable source.

Mark your circle on the ground by securing the end of a piece of string in the ground in the center of the circle with a net or tent peg. Hold the other end and, using a temporary spray paint, rotate around the center to mark the circle's outline.

Position your stones. Look at each stone carefully and "read" it before you place it. They will all be different, and each may suggest where they would like to stand and in which direction they should face.

Dig a shallow hole at each stone's position and move them into place.

Once stones are in place, if the circle is big enough, sit in the center and imagine an invisible wall rising all around you to form a dome. If the circle is smaller, place a candle in the center and visualize the dome. This hemisphere of energy will stay there. You now have your own sacred space.

Hold a ritual to "open" the circle (see page 18).

A fire ritual

A fire ceremony connects us to our ancestors who gathered around fires to cook, keep warm, and to dance. In Shamanic practice, fire is said to provide a way to let go of what is not needed and replace it with what is. By releasing old patterns and habits, you create an opportunity to be reborn, a personal transformation.

Choose an auspicious day for your ritual. A full moon or a new moon are always powerful, as are the eight festivals of the Wheel of the Year—Beltane (May 1) in particular is associated with fire.

Make a "spirit arrow," by choosing a small stick and writing what you want to be rid of on it.

Cast your circle (see page 18) either around your firepit or with your fire bowl in the center.

Light the sacred fire by placing kindling in the form of a cross at the base of the firepit or bowl.

Build a tepee of small pieces of dry wood over the kindling. Fill with paper and more kindling. Keep it small; this is a ceremonial fire, not a bonfire night blaze. Light the fire.

Chant, dance, or just sit and watch the flames.

Make the fire friendly with three offerings of olive oil. The first offering honors the four directions. Sprinkle oil on the fire and allow it to burn. The second offering is to honor heaven and earth. Sprinkle oil on the fire and allow it to burn. The third offering honors all those present, including spirits of the land and ancestors. Sprinkle oil on the fire and allow it to burn.

Pass your hands briefly through the smoke (safely above the flames!) and draw the energy of the fire into your belly, heart, and forehead.

Gently lower your spirit arrow into the fire.

Wait until the fire burns out and your spirit arrow has gone.

Close the circle.

The magic of smoke

Ethereal, aromatic, and transient, smoke has a magic all of its own. As it billows from a fire, then drifts away into the trees and beyond, it resembles something otherworldly and mysterious. Maybe it's because of these properties that smoke has been used in the spiritual practices of many different cultures and faiths since ancient times.

When using smoke in a ritual, it is important to look to your own culture first. Commercialization of Native American smoking or "smudging" customs has led to careless and offensive cultural appropriation. I prefer to tap into the Scottish Celtic tradition of "saining," whereby smoke from aromatic plants such as juniper is used in blessing ceremonies, often in conjunction with the sprinkling of water. One simple ritual is to fumigate the house with a branch of smoldering rosemary, then fling open the windows to let fresh air in.

A SMOKE RITUAL

Make a couple of bundles of aromatic plants to burn in advance. Loose, dried petals and sticks that can be thrown on the fire also work. Choose plants that match your intention (see opposite for examples). This is the time to state (or think) about what you want, whether it's healing for yourself or another person, a specific wish, general well-being or peace, clearing negativity, or whatever is your most pressing need.

Open a sacred space. You could Declare peace in the quarters (the cardinal compass points), call in the five elements, or cast a circle around where the fire will blaze.

Build the fire intentionally (see page 78). Keep it small to minimize air pollution. A few logs blazing in a firepit or fire bowl in the garden is perfect.

Light your fire and tend it until you have a good blaze to smolder your bundles.

Place your bundles in front of you. Bless them with the elements, then invite the elements in to help.

State your intention as you offer the bundles to the fire.

Watch as the bundles burn. See if any messages come to you within the flames. As the fire burns, picture the wind taking the smoke to where you want it to go. This is also the time to sing, dance, and drum if that feels right.

Close the space by circling it as you thank the elements.

Allow the fire to burn out naturally and allow the magic to happen.

AROMATIC PLANTS TO GROW AND BURN

Certain aromatic plants release scented smoke when dried and burned and have magical properties. Grow a selection in the garden so that you always have some handy to use in rituals. Depending on the plant, use either the leaves or small branches or sticks. Sprinkle onto a fire or gather in bundles.

Juniper (*Juniperus communis*): throw small dried branches on to the fire for protection and to clear negative energy. The smoke is also said to boost psychic powers.

Lavender (*Lavandula*): invites friendly spirits into your sacred space and cleanses it.

Mugwort (*Artemisia vulgaris*): mugwort is a "messenger plant"—the smoke from its dried leaves is said to help connection with nature and encourage lucid dreaming.

Pine (*Pinus*): gather pine cones on Midsummer Day when the seeds are still in place. When dry, burn on the fire to release cleansing smoke. Pine needles can also be used; when burned they are also said to reverse bad spells.

Rosemary (*Rosmarinus officinalis*): when burned, rosemary emits cleansing and purifying smoke that helps with energy flow, strengthens the memory, and protects the space.

Vervain (*Verbena officinalis*): the smoke from bundles of vervain dispels unrequited love. It also brings balance, inner strength, and peace.

Juniper

Mugwort

Rosemary

Vervain

CHAPTER 5

Earth

Working with Mother Earth

Of all the elements Earth is, unsurprisingly, of great importance to gardeners. Once you have a garden of your own, you pay it more attention. Rather than an annoying, filthy thing that dogs and people bring into the house, disregarded because it is beneath your feet, you see earth as it really is—the source of all living things.

Urban living has distanced us from Earth. Hidden under buildings, parking lots, and sidewalks, it is only glimpsed at the periphery of our lives. We buy bags of potting compost to fill containers without paying much attention to what it contains, spray weedkiller on the soil without thinking what it could be doing beneath the surface, and dig and rotavate our plots without considering the structure of the soil and the creatures that inhabit it.

My garden is organic, not just because I grow vegetables and want them (and me) to be as healthy as possible, but because I can't bear the thought of poisoning Mother Earth. Sometimes this resolve is tested as I repeatedly pull dandelions from cracks in the paving, or despair at the aphids on my fava (broad) beans, but so far, I have not wavered. I try not to dig the vegetable garden, practicing the "No Dig" method which does not disrupt the soil structure, leaving microorganisms, fungi, and worms to work their magic. And any compost I buy to sow seeds and pot up plants is peat-free. (Peat is the earth's carbon store and should be treasured, especially at this time of climate crisis.)

This, I feel, is the least I can do to repay Mother Earth for all she does for us. As human beings, we are the stewards of the land. There are many instances where we have failed in our responsibilities to care for it—which makes looking after our own small patch ever more important.

THE MAGIC OF EARTH

Earth, as you might expect, is the most stable and grounding of all the elements. It also represents fertility, birth, and rebirth—Mother Earth is the source of all life. As well as symbolizing beginnings, it is also the element of endings—we all return to the earth when we die.

Call on Earth when doing magical work around wealth, sexuality, family, home, and growth. As gardeners we are always near Earth, so maintain close contact with it when carrying out earth-based rituals and spells. If the weather prevents this, have a pot of earth from your garden handy to use inside.

GROUNDING

Some people believe that walking barefoot in their garden will connect them to electrical charges in the earth. Called "grounding," this is said to improve certain health conditions such as chronic pain and cardiovascular disease. However, it has not been proven and the scientific community remains skeptical.

Personally, I think walking barefoot on the ground has its own, simple benefits and pleasures which cannot be measured. They are more about understanding our relationship with Earth than bringing about miraculous health treatments.

Earth correspondences

The element of Earth is associated with the following things—known as correspondences—which are handy to refer to when planning and planting your magical garden.

Colour: green.

How to use: there is no end to the ways you can introduce green into your garden, from herbaceous perennials to flowering shrubs, trees, and grasses. To ensure you have some greenery all year round, look for evergreen plants like *Fatsia japonica*, with its shiny, green, palm-shaped leaves, or ivy which has green leaves all year. You could also create a "green garden" of plants of different shades of green, with variously shaped leaves. It's amazing how many variations there are of this one color, and how soothing and calming it is.

Direction: north.

How to use: gardens that face north are in shade for most of the day, as the house blocks the sun. Rather than despair at the gloom, embrace it instead and make a fernery. Ferns will thrive as long as the soil is good enough. There are a great many different types of ferns to assemble into a lush, green bank.

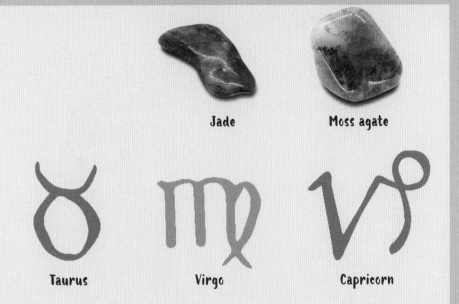

Jade

Moss agate

Taurus

Virgo

Capricorn

Time: midnight.

How to use: this is the time to head out into the garden for an earth-based ritual or to cast spells around fertility, abundance, or work.

Witch's tool: pentacle.

How to use: taking the five-pointed star within a circle as a template, create a mosaic in pebbles, or plant a herb garden with different herbs within each of the points, and a taller herb such as bay in the center.

Crystals: jade, pyrite, moss agate, tourmaline.

How to use: place one of these crystals on your outdoor altar during rituals or spellcasting.

Zodiac signs: Taurus, Virgo, Capricorn.

Tarot suit: pentacles.

Goddesses associated with the land

Call upon these goddesses in earth-based rituals.

Danu, Celtic goddess of the earth

In Irish mythology, Danu restored magic to the people by appearing as a mist to teach them skills and impart wisdom. The mist is thought to be her loving embrace. She is also associated with music and poetry and is often represented by the Celtic three-spiral symbol, the Triskele.

Gaia, Greek goddess of the earth

The personification of Earth in Greek mythology and the mother of all life, Gaia has come to represent the spiritual embodiment of the earth, or Earth itself in modern neopagan belief.

Prithvi: Hindu and Buddhist goddess of the earth

The word *prithvi* is also the Sanskrit name for the "earth." With the god of the sky, Dyaus, Prithvi created the world. She is depicted with four arms, three of which hold a lotus in each hand, with a water vessel held in the other.

Pachamama: Inca goddess of the earth

A fertility goddess of the indigenous people of the Andes, Pachamama oversees the harvest, embodies mountains, and causes earthquakes.

What lies beneath you: the wonder of soil

Living in towns and cities can separate us from the earth beneath our feet. Often it is dismissed as "dirt" and a nuisance. It is paved over, artificial grass is laid on top of it, or it is flooded with chemicals to kill weeds or boost crops.

Cultivating my garden has made me realize how vital it is to "see" the earth and to take care of it. After I have heaped garden compost on the vegetable beds in winter, the soil pleasingly wriggles with worms in spring. Difficult areas of heavy clay have responded to the addition of organic matter and plants now really thrive there.

The magic of soil is underappreciated and still relatively unknown. Rather than being a dull mass of ground rock and dead plants, what lies beneath our feet is a rich and diverse ecosystem. It is home to several hundred thousand small animals and fungi. It teems with bacteria—the earthy smell loved by gardeners is the scent of the compounds they produce. Soil should not be underestimated or disregarded. As writer and environmental activist George Monbiot writes: "Soil is the thin cushion between rock and air on which human life depends, yet we treat it like dirt."

As you plan your magical garden, take some time to look closely at your soil. It may be heavy clay, sandy, or a mixture of both. You can buy soil-testing kits in garden centers that will help you with this. The type of soil you have will affect what you can grow in your garden: some plants thrive in nutrient-rich clay, for example, while others will perish.

Also look around at the geology of the land nearby and tap into that. I discovered that over 450,000 years ago, a substantial river once flowed near my garden which deposited sand and coarse gravel as it went. This has given me a greater understanding of the local topography and of the makeup of the soil. Discovering underlying rock formations can be tricky in cities and towns, but there are geological maps that will help you see beneath the paving and the buildings to what lies deeper.

The magic of compost

That so much that nourishes, soothes, and delights us springs from the soil is down to Mother Earth. One of the ways we can work alongside her is to make our own compost. Compost is basically another word for humus—not the chickpea dip but decomposed plant matter. It helps retain moisture, creates good soil structure, and provides nutrients. It is nature's way of dealing with its own waste and it is awesome.

Compost never fails to amaze me. You take a load of unwanted smelly vegetable peelings and garden waste, heap it up, and, with a little care and attention, it turns into a wonderful, dark brown organic material that smells like the essence of Earth. The compost bins in my garden do this with very little attention from me, although I know if I tried a little harder the results would be quicker, contain fewer sticks, and require less sieving.

THIS IS THE BEST METHOD TO GET GOOD RESULTS

You need the **right combination of materials** containing carbon and nitrogen: dry stuff like cardboard and dry leaves (carbon) mixed with vegetable scraps, lawn mowings, or plant clippings, for example, to supply nitrogen.

Cut or shred everything into smaller pieces. That way it will decompose more quickly.

Don't add meat, fish, dairy products, or cat and dog droppings. That will make the compost stink. Restrict what you add to plant material.

Turn the compost every so often to introduce oxygen, so bacteria can get to work.

If your garden isn't big enough for a compost heap, consider a Bokashi composting system which you can keep in the kitchen. This Japanese method layers kitchen scraps with sawdust in a special container, which is shut when full and allowed to ferment for 10–14 days. This creates a liquid that can be drained off and used as fertilizer.

Magical trees

The first thing I look for in a garden, no matter how small, is a tree. A garden without a tree lacks soul. It also lacks somewhere shady to sit in summer, a perch for birds, a leafy canopy that tumbles colorfully to the ground in the fall, and a home for countless insects. Trees are the wise elders of the plant world and as such should be treated not only with gratitude for all they provide, but also with respect for all they know.

My two favorite trees in my garden are a silver birch that shimmers in the sun and shivers in the breeze, and a wild service tree which is native to this area, but rare elsewhere. On the boundary of the garden there is also an elderly and beautiful oak, which I can't believe is temporarily under my care (it is certain to outlive me).

The trees in our gardens not only provide joy for generations to come, but also offer contact with an awesome and mysterious energy. Every culture has tales and myths associated with its own trees. In some indigenous communities, individual trees are regarded as having their own spirit which must be courted and protected to bring blessings to the people.

THE RIGHT TREE

Choose a tree, or trees for your garden carefully. Don't just rely on internet searches; go out and find one in three dimensions, then see if you have a connection with it. Also consider practical matters such as how high and wide it grows, and whether it has blossom in the spring and colorful leaves in the fall. The first thing I planted in my garden was a rowan or mountain ash (*Sorbus aucuparia*), because it is said to protect the house and its occupants from evil. So far, so good!

The following trees all come with magical or spiritual associations and are worth considering for your magical garden.

The King of the Forest: common oak (*Quercus robur*)

With its distinctive paw-shaped leaves, acorns, and gnarly bark, the oak is easy to identify. What I love about it most, though, are its wide, welcoming branches that look as though they are about to give you a hug. There is one oak I am particularly fond of that my dog Peggy and I pass on walks. We always stop and sit for a moment beneath its boughs to feel the benefit of its sheltering and protective canopy. It even stills the boisterous and bouncy Peggy.

The oak's great size and presence are synonymous with strength and steadfastness, characteristics that often feature in folk customs and mythology. The Green Man, for example, frequently has oak leaves growing from his mouth. It is an important tree for druids (the word *druid* can be translated as "oak knowledge" or "oak seer"), who meet in sacred groves of oak trees to perform their ceremonies.

Oak trees are a little large for most gardens, so I like to pot up an acorn or two in some potting compost. Miniature trees result, which can be potted on as they get larger, and maybe even planted in a woodland one day.

Walk around the trunk of an oak and any ailment will be carried off by the birds. A Welsh custom is to rub an oak with the palm of your hand on Midsummer Day. Then you will stay well all year.

The Queen of the Forest: common ash (*Fraxinus excelsior*)

This most elegant of trees is recognizable in winter by its velvety buds and clusters of seeds called keys. In summer, the leaves move in the direction of the sun, and in the fall the leaves stay green when they drop to the ground. Sadly, in the UK the ash is in peril due to a disease called ash dieback—all the more reason to treasure it now.

Ash is a tree of enchantment and healing, shrouded in mystical associations. Wands made from ash branches date back to the 1st century CE (one was found on Anglesey in Wales) and the wood from the tree was thought to protect against bad fairies. In Norse mythology, it was known as Yggdrasil, or the World Tree, which spanned the realms of Heaven, Earth, and the Underworld.

Put ash leaves under your pillow to encourage prophetic dreams. Ash keys (seeds) are thought to keep evil away.

The White Lady of the Woods: silver birch (*Betula pendula*)

With its ghostly white bark and dangling, twiggy branches that shiver in the breeze, the silver birch is the perfect tree for a magical garden. I planted a Himalayan birch (*Betula utilis* var. *jacquemontii*) when I lived in London. It was a daily delight with its dangling catkins in the fall and its chalk-white, skeletal branches exposed in winter. It also doesn't get too big so is good for smaller gardens. In the wild, silver birch often grows in a clearing in a wood—hence its name, white lady of the woods.

Make a besom (broomstick) from its twiggy branches and sweep the boundaries of your property to keep everyone safe. Maypoles and Yule logs are also made from silver birch trunks.

The Ancient One: common yew (*Taxus baccata*)

The churchyard in my village, like many churchyards, has two ancient yews. One is hollowed out (yews rot from the inside) and the cavity is big enough to stand in. I like to do that whenever I pass it. There's nothing like being inside an ancient tree to connect you with nature and the past. I don't know how old that tree is, but some yews have lived for thousands of years. One of the reasons for their long life is their regenerative properties: a dangling branch can take root and form a trunk to support the main tree. It's because of this ability to renew itself that the yew is associated with death and resurrection.

In Irish mythology, the yew is one of the five sacred Guardian Trees said to be brought from the Otherworld by a tall stranger—the others are oak, ash, apple, and hazel.

Rather than plant a yew tree in your garden, consider using it as a hedging plant. It is evergreen, densely foliated, and can be clipped into interesting shapes as it grows.

Don't even think about eating yew berries or making an infusion from its leaves. Every part of this plant is poisonous.

The Bountiful Beauty: apple (*Malus domestica*)

There is little that makes me as happy as seeing the apple trees in the orchard afroth with blossom in mid-spring. It is a sign that spring has arrived. In the fall, the same trees will be heavy with apples. The metamorphosis from bare twigs to orbs of crunchy fruit always amazes me. It feels a lot like magic.

Perhaps it's this mysterious transformation that has led to apples appearing in many folk stories and fairy tales from *Sleeping Beauty* to the Arthurian legends to the story of Adam and Eve in the Bible.

Any magical garden, whatever the size, should have a fruit tree. There are many dwarf varieties that can be grown in pots. Look for self-pollinating varieties grown on dwarfing or semi-dwarfing rootstocks. As well as apples, you could also grow pears, quinces, plums, damsons, or peaches, all of which have dwarf varieties that grow well in containers.

Cut an apple in half and a secret will be revealed: the seeds are arranged in a perfect pentangle.

The Wizard's Tree: rowan (*Sorbus aucuparia*)

This is a personal favorite of mine and I have two in my garden. One was there when I moved in, and I planted the other in the top of my fairy mound (see page 107). I like to give a rowan (also called mountain ash as they thrive on rocky hilltops) as a housewarming present to friends to protect the home and everyone in it from danger. (Its old Celtic name is *fid na ndruad* which means "wizard's tree.") Wood from a rowan was once used to stir milk to prevent it from curdling and made into a pocket charm against rheumatism.

A rowan is an excellent choice for smaller gardens, as it won't get too big. It also has frothy white blossom in spring, followed by cheery red berries in the fall.

Make a divining rod from a rowan branch. You'll need a forked one for it to be effective.

The May Tree: hawthorn (*Crataegus monogyna*)

The hawthorn is associated with Beltane (May 1), as this is when its mass of white blossom appears. Maypoles were once made from its timber, as were garlands. However, it was believed to be unlucky to bring any into the house. Hawthorn has long been considered a magical tree in Ireland, and fairies were thought to live in its branches. Dense and thorny, it makes a good hedge, but its white blossom and red fruit (haws) also make it an attractive standalone tree for your magical garden. Although fairies aren't guaranteed, it will become home to a great many insects, while its haws will provide nourishment for migrating birds to power their flight onward.

Include some hawthorn blossom in a spring wedding bouquet. It is symbolic of love and will bring blessings to the marriage.

The herb garden

My priority when creating any garden is to find a patch to grow herbs. I am much happier once a selection of these useful and attractive plants is in the ground and flourishing. In my current garden, I dug up a patch of lawn by the vegetable beds to plant with herbs. There are also other herbs in pots by the back door—in easy snipping distance for cooking and making herbal remedies.

A herb garden also forms a connection with women herbalists of the past who practiced "wort cunning." *Wort* is the Saxon word for "herb" (and lives on in the name of the herb St John's wort). "Cunning" refers to knowledge of the healing and magical properties of herbs and the skills to make use of this knowledge. Wort cunning was essential to women who worked as midwives or administered herbal remedies. In the 16th century, many of these women were tortured, tried, and executed during the brutal witch trials. I like to think about these women as I tend my little herb garden. How unfortunate for them to be born at that time, and how fortunate we are to be alive now.

You can imagine then how pleased I was to find records dating from around 1400 of a witch living in my village. Called Amisia Daniel, but known as The Old Gander, she preferred pigs for company, "made use of sorcery," and lived in a "hovel." Her home is long gone, and the land it stood on is now plowed to grow beet. I wonder if Amisia ever grew herbs there and if she brewed up concoctions in her hovel.

One of the great things about herbs is that you don't need much space to grow them. A windowsill or a sunny doorstep will provide the perfect conditions for a few containers brimming with herbal favorites. They also grow happily without much intervention. Provide them with the right soil and a sunny position and off they go. Overleaf are six of my favorites, which I grow for culinary and magical purposes:

Bay (*Laurus nobilis*): clipped into a lollipop-shape, a little bay tree makes an ornamental addition to the herb garden and has many culinary uses (my favorite is a few leaves added to a hearty stew). It also features in Greek and Roman mythology and has been used in traditional customs for centuries.

Magical use: burn dried and crushed bay leaves to encourage visions and psychic insights.

Bay

Mint (*Mentha*): there are many varieties of mint to choose from, but the two I prefer are Corsican mint (*Mentha requienii*), which is low growing and has a punchy, minty aroma, and chocolate peppermint (*Mentha* x *piperita* f. *citrata* "Chocolate"), which smells like After Eight confectionary.

Magical use: mint can be used to ease a fractious relationship. Serve mint tea to an argumentative person to ease the situation. It is also a good memory booster and is delicious on new potatoes.

Mint

Myrtle (*Myrtus communis*): this is such a pretty shrub—it has fragrant white flowers, purple berries, and its leaves smell gorgeous when crushed. It makes a striking centerpiece in any herb garden.

Magical use: sprinkle myrtle flowers and leaves in the bath to give your sex life a boost, or put a few sprigs in a bud vase beside the bed for the same purpose.

Myrtle

Rosemary (*Rosmarinus officinalis*): there is a rosemary bush outside my back door, so it's very handy to cut a few sprigs and add them to a pot of hot water for a refreshing drink. It smells divine as I brush past it on the way out and has pretty lavender flowers that are loved by bees. It is also a powerful magical plant.

Magical use: rosemary can be used as an ingredient in many charms and spells. I like to use it to remember those who have died by placing a sprig in front of an old photo at Samhain (October 31). Give a rosemary plant as a present to forge a strong and supportive friendship.

Rue (*Ruta graveolens*): along with vervain, rue was often cited as a herb used by witches in witch trial records. For this reason alone, it is worth planting. It also has attractive, fern-like leaves and frilly yellow flowers.

Magical use: to protect things precious to you that may cause envy in others. Dried and hung in cloth bags, it can be used as an insect repellent.

Woad (*Isatis tinctoria*): I planted this herb since it can be made into a blue dye and because it has an intriguing history as the body paint of Pictish warriors. I didn't realize, however, how big it grows: its yellow flowers tower over the other herbs. This is not a huge problem, though—they are lovely as cut flowers.

Magical use: use in protection magic or as a poultice to ease inflammation.

Woad

THE PHYSIC GARDEN

A great place to get inspiration for what herbs to grow is a physic garden. Here you will find plants and herbs grouped according to the ailment they are used to treat. This is very handy when it comes to choosing what to grow for herbal remedies.

The origins of physic gardens were medieval monasteries where monks grew herbs such as sage, rosemary, mint, thyme, and borage to prepare ointments, infusions, and purgatives. The first physic garden was founded in 1621, at the Oxford Botanic Garden in the UK, to grow plants for medicinal use, and the most famous one is the four-acre (1.6 hectares) Chelsea Physic Garden in London.

A FEW HERBAL ASSOCIATIONS

To foster love: apple, basil, dill, jasmine, lavender, thyme.

To encourage wealth: comfrey, ginger, honeysuckle.

To protect things that matter: bay, clove, fennel, witch hazel.

To maintain good health: coriander, knotweed, parsley.

To boost fertility: geranium, mustard, peach, poppy.

To cultivate happiness: catnip, celandine, hawthorn, marjoram.

To build courage: borage, mullein, yarrow.

Honeysuckle

Shaping the earth

The countryside around my garden is soft and rolling. In the distance are the Malvern Hills, and between there and here are smaller hills descending in height as they get closer, like waves tumbling to the shore. Most of these hills are wooded, and little streams whose banks brim with wild garlic and bluebells in the spring, run through their valleys. Lanes rather than roads connect the villages and, apart from a few enormous tractors thundering past, it is a peaceful place.

I wanted my garden to echo this landscape in some way. Instead of a pristine place of ornamental borders and clipped hedges, I wanted something wilder, softer, more magical. One of the first things I did to attempt this was to remove a rickety old garden swing to make room for a fairy mound: a little hillock planted with wild flowers (see page 109).

Thinking of the garden in three dimensions rather than as a flat area of lawn and

borders, has liberated my thinking. To inspire me, I looked at some amazing, much bigger gardens. Charles Jencks's Garden of Cosmic Speculation in Scotland, for example, is a series of landforms sculpted and carved from the earth—a fascinating and mystical landscape inspired by cosmology. Slumbering in the Lost Gardens of Heligan in Cornwall, southwestern England, is the Mud Maid, a figure lying on, and in, the earth. Her appearance changes with the seasons as the plants that cover her come and go. The biggest of the lot is Glastonbury Tor in Somerset, also in southwestern England, which, some say, has been shaped into a three-dimensional labyrinth. I am keeping that in mind for my next project: a landform shaped by a spiral.

In the meantime, I have my little modest fairy mound. I'm happy with how it reflects the shape of the hills and connects the garden with the world beyond the fence. It is also, of course, a home for any fairies and nature spirits, or devas (see opposite), who live in the garden.

DEVAS AND NATURE SPIRITS

The term "devas" was first applied to nature spirits by Eileen and Peter Caddy and their friend Dorothy Maclean, of the Findhorn Foundation in Scotland. They credited their abundant vegetable garden, grown on barren soil, to a collaboration between themselves and the devas, who, they believed, were responsible for keeping everything alive. Every plant has its own type of deva who looks after it. *Deva* is a Sanskrit word that is similar in meaning to "angel."

Another belief, animism, credits all natural phenomena, including human beings, animals, and plants, but also rocks, lakes, mountains, and the weather, with sharing one soul or spirit that energizes them. The ancient Celts are said to have been animists, and this belief system is still practiced in regions of Africa, the Arctic, and Asian Myanmar.

MAKING A FAIRY MOUND

Any garden, however small, has room for a fairy mound. Simply pile up some earth—how much and how high is up to you—then either sow it with wildflower seed or cover it with wildflower turf. I went for the turf option, which was very easy to lay but more expensive than seed. It also meant I had no control over what plants came up, so have since been weeding out some of the more thuggish ones and replacing with prettier, smaller varieties. (I figure the fairies prefer these.) You approach the fairy mound across the lawn and through the moon gate, so it draws you toward it. Which brings me to the importance of creating a journey through your magical garden.

The path to magic

How you move through a garden is an important part of creating a magical space. You want to create a journey of discovery which unfolds as you go, a little like life itself. The simplest way to enhance and direct this journey is to create a path.

Paths are often overlooked in the greater scheme of things, but they are as important as showier elements and link them together like beads on a necklace. The pace of the garden is set by its paths: the straighter the path, the faster you travel. Who wants to be hurried along a straight track to the shed when you could wander along a meandering route, stopping along the way to admire the firepit or smell the flowers?

To work out the path's direction, walk the route a few times to establish a "desire line," that is, the path most traveled that takes you where you want to go. Then consider what materials to use. I have a gravel path alongside the garage and a turf one that winds through the flower beds. The gravel one is harder to look after as it needs constant weeding. The simplest and loveliest path of all, however, is one sinuous line mown through long grass. Although this suits large areas of land, preferably planted as a meadow, it works on smaller patches, too. Once you have established the paths, the rest of the garden will fall into place. Well-positioned paths will also ensure that the flow of chi (see page 57) is unobstructed.

Animal guides

We are not the only sentient creatures on the planet; we share this ability with other animals. It is important to live harmoniously with other creatures and nowhere more so than in our magical gardens. By watching the behavior of animals and birds and noticing their comings and goings, we connect with a world beyond our own, and by caring for them we practice compassion and tenderness. They can also teach us things about ourselves that had not been evident before, and some are even considered to have magical powers.

Four hens roam about my garden, getting under my feet as I dig and squawking loudly when they lay an egg. In the morning, going to the hen house and finding speckled brown eggs lying in the straw feels incredible every time. How a perfectly formed (and very tasty) egg emerges from the bodies of my feathered friends is astonishing. Keeping hens has enabled me to get to know them really well, from their strange, prehistoric-looking claws, to their comical and wide-ranging clucks and cackles. It has also made me step up and take responsibility for their welfare: shutting them in at night, supplying food, making sure they have water, and that the hen house is clean.

Any garden, however small, can welcome and encourage other living beings. A feeder full of seeds or nuts will attract a daily crowd of fluttering and pecking birds. A pond, however small, will bring a crowd of water-loving insects and amphibians (I was delighted to find newts in mine). All living things, including most importantly our pets, have qualities and characteristics that we can learn from. Some people even have a magical connection with their animals.

SPIRIT AND POWER ANIMALS

Some witches and pagan practitioners have a particular affinity with a certain animal and contact it for guidance and in rituals. Here are five that are favored:

The cat: black cats in particular are associated with magic and have been since ancient times, cropping up in legends and folklore in many different cultures. In ancient Egypt, they were associated with the goddesses Bast and Sekhmet. In Japan, a figurine called a *maneki-neko* will draw money into the house with its raised and waving paw.

The crow: often seen as harbingers of doom, I prefer to see these clever and resourceful birds as messengers. What they are trying to say is open to interpretation, though some use them as a method of divination.

The owl: perhaps it's because of the owl's ability to rotate its neck through 270 degrees, or because of its ghostly nocturnal habits, that it features in many superstitions, myths, and legends. The sight of a barn owl flying low out of the woods is truly enchanting and stops me in my tracks every time.

The rabbit: called on in magical work to boost sexual energy, especially around the spring equinox (Ostara) because of the female's ability to produce many offspring.

The bee: often associated with health and wealth in superstition and folklore. In Celtic mythology, a bee was a messenger between this world and the spirit realm.

Earth spells and rituals

A GROUNDING RITUAL

If you spend a lot of time in front of a computer or generally living in your head rather than your body, this simple exercise will tune you into the Earth element and bring head and body back into alignment. I love this ritual because it helps to quieten busy minds and soothe anxious souls.

Take a candle and go into the garden to find a place that feels comfortable and safe.

Light the candle and lie on the ground. Keep as close to the earth as possible—so don't lie on paving or asphalt if you can avoid it.

Breathe deeply, inflating your lungs from the bottom to the top.

Exhale fully, emptying your lungs of air.

Do this three times, and as you do so, visualize your body sinking into the ground.

As you inhale, imagine your body receiving goodness from the earth and let its weight be absorbed and supported by it.

As you exhale, release all your worries and anxieties into the earth.

Imagine you have roots snaking out from your back and into the earth, keeping you grounded and steady.

Allow yourself to be held as long as it is comfortable. Ask yourself what else you can let go of, and release that, too.

When the time feels right, blow out the candle.

Hold the calm feeling as you return indoors.

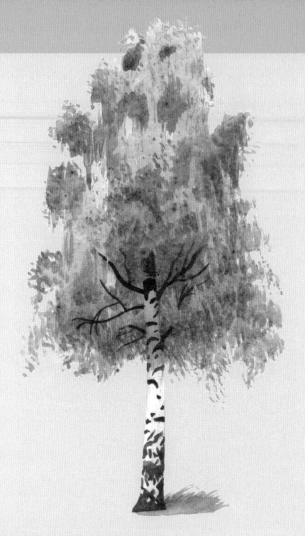

A SIMPLE BIRCH SPELL

First find a piece of birch bark. Birch trees often peel—it's one of the attractive things about them—so it is easy to remove a little bit. Don't take too much, though: you don't want to damage the tree. Find a birch twig and, using its tip, write a promise or a wish on the bark. Keep the piece of bark safe and wait until your wish is fulfilled. Then thank the spirit of the tree. (Gratitude is important in spells.)

You could also include a little birch bark or dried leaf in an incense blend and burn it at the start of any important journey or stage in your life.

FLASH RITUAL: THANK A TREE

Go and find your favorite tree. If it's not in the garden, walk mindfully toward it, thinking of it as you go. Make the tree your destination and your walk a pilgrimage. When you arrive, place the palm of your hand against its trunk and hold it there for a few moments. Notice its calming effect. Thank the tree and retrace your steps, while keeping that feeling of calmness in your heart.

WAYS TO CONNECT WITH EARTH

- **Plunge your hands into fresh soil or potting compost**. Hold the earthy material and, as you do so, appreciate all it does to keep us alive and well.

- **Walk barefoot in the mud or on grass**. Relish the feeling of the ground on the soles of your feet.

- **Go out into the country and find a boulder**. Sit on the boulder and connect with its energy. Focus on its great age and its substance.

- **Lie under a tree in full leaf**. Feel the ground supporting you and keeping you stable. Look up through the leaves to the sky. Think about the Tree of Life and how the roots, trunk, and canopy of the tree connect the underworld, the earth, and the celestial world.

CHAPTER 6

Air

Sensing air all around

Air is the one thing we all have plenty of in our gardens: it is all around us after all. It is also inside our bodies as breath. Unlike the three physical elements, however, we can't see Air unless it interacts with them—causing a fire to combust into life and extinguishing it, rustling the leaves of a tree, scattering seed, or oxygenating ponds. It is everywhere and part of everything, yet isn't visible.

We might not be able to see air, but we can sense it. It is the feeling of the wind on our skin and the movement of clouds in the sky. It is the scent of flowers carried on a breeze or the forest floor after a shower. It is the sound of leaves stirring as a storm begins. It is an exhalation of breath as we climb a hill or watch a sunset.

In traditional Chinese culture *qi*, which translates literally as "air" or "breath," is the vital force in all of us and in everything, and which must not be blocked but allowed to flow easily. This is realized in the practice of feng shui (see page 57) and can be applied to gardens by considering the placing of gates and garden furniture, and the shape of paths (among other things). In Sanskrit, *vata* is the word for "air" or "wind," and is the name of one the three *doshas* (energies) in Ayurvedic medicine, where it is said to control movements in the body such as blood flow, digestion, and breath. It also has an association with fairies and other ethereal creatures who fly about on the eddies of the wind, particularly at those times of the year when the barrier between this world and the next is the thinnest. Communication with these Air Elementals, which are also called sylphs, can be carried out by whistling or singing.

I am always conscious of air in my garden, mainly through the shape and movement of the wind. It can be fierce and destructive during winter storms or a soft, gentle breeze, welcome on a hot day spent gardening. I also connect with it through the different smells and sounds in the garden, from the comforting chuckle of my hens to the waft of lavender as I brush past on the way to the compost heap.

THE MAGIC OF AIR

The element of Air symbolizes the intellect, creativity, communication, and psychic abilities. Call on it to build clairvoyance, during meditation centered around the breath (see page 138), and when searching for inspiration or boosting creativity. Use it to practice conscious breathing before magic work to feel centered and grounded.

THREE WAYS TO CONNECT WITH AIR IN THE GARDEN

1 Sit comfortably under a tree when it is in full leaf (so not in winter!). Notice how the wind moves through the tree, causing leaves to flutter and branches to bow. Notice what sound the wind makes as it passes through the boughs.

2 Lie on the ground on a summer's day and watch the clouds change shape and drift across the sky. Although they may appear static, you will soon notice that currents in the air constantly move them. Often clouds may take on the form of something familiar before that too morphs and is blown away. Some witches use what they see for divinatory purposes.

3 Notice how the wind feels on your skin. How a gentle summer breeze blows on your bare arms, for example, or a frisky gust ruffles your hair on a windy day. Try to imagine the shape of the wind and picture how it is moving around you.

Air correspondences

The element of Air is associated with the following things—known as correspondences—which can be incorporated when you are planning and planting your magical garden.

Colors: yellow, white, pale colors generally.
How to use: create an airy bed with scented plants (see page 87). Many white plants have an ethereal quality at dusk and emit a gorgeous scent. Try star jasmine (*Trachelospermum jasminoides*), which has pretty, white, fragrant flowers, or the tobacco plant (*Nicotiana sylvestris*), a statuesque annual whose long white blooms have an intense fragrance in the evening.

Direction: East.
How to use: East-facing borders are shady, cool places where sun-loving plants won't flourish. Create a lush, green bed instead with plants that prefer partial shade. *Viburnum opulus*, for example, has pom-poms of white flowers followed by red berries. Hang a wind chime to capture passing breezes.

Crystals: blue fluorite, citrine, labradorite, moonstone, topaz, zircon.

Viburnum

Blue fluorite

Labradorite

Moonstone

Zircon

Gemini

Libra

Aquarius

Hazel

How to use: Air crystals support clarity and lucidity, including spiritual visions. Place one on your outdoor altar during a ritual or when scrying.

Magical tool: the wand.
How to use: make your own wand from a tree that has meaning for you. Hazel and willow are nice, light, and whippy.

Zodiac signs: Gemini, Libra, Aquarius.

The sounds of the garden

"I hear the wind among the trees
Playing celestial symphonies;
I see the branches downward bent,
Like keys of some great instrument."

Henry Wadsworth Longfellow from "A Day of Sunshine"

Sound travels on the air and nowhere more so than outdoors in the garden. A garden with no sound at all feels like a dead space. Too many hard surfaces or impenetrable evergreen hedges can flatten or obliterate the gentle whisper of the wind or the call of a blackbird.

What you hear in your garden can affect what you experience, but it can be hard to control, especially in the city where the sound of a neighbor's barbecue party or passing traffic sometimes drowns out gentler noises. Fortunately, there are ways to introduce peaceful, meditative sounds to turn your garden into a restful sanctuary.

My garden is, on the whole, quiet. That was one of the reasons I chose to live in the country. I hadn't realized, however, that enormous tractors would rattle past the front of the house on a regular basis, or that a neighbor a field away would hold incredibly loud firework parties. Happily, these are sporadic events. Instead, I have learned to tune into the song of the trees as the wind rushes through them, am learning how to identify birds by their song, and have chosen plants for their rustling sound as they move in summer breezes.

THE SONG OF THE TREES

Since I have learned to train my ear to certain sounds, my hearing is a little sharper. With this new "mindful" listening, I have discovered that each tree makes its own distinctive sound. Wind rushing through the leaves of the silver birch sounds like waves rolling onto a shingle beach. The old oak tree, however, makes a deeper, throatier noise which can become a boom when the wind is strong. This "susurration"—the sound of leaves in the wind—is deeply restful and the perfect soundtrack to meditation or a nap beneath its boughs.

All magical gardens, however small, need a tree. Even if you only have a backyard, you can plant a small tree like a rowan or a fruit tree in a container. My potted fruit tree was—and this is not an exaggeration—a daily joy. I plan to plant more trees to supplement what I already have here in the country. In the meantime, I head off to the woods whenever I can to sit beneath the pine trees as they "whisper together and bend in the wind" (a lyric from "Witches Hat" by The Incredible String Band).

BIRDS IN THE TREES

Birdsong is the music of the garden and fills it with life, delight, and an ever-changing, unpredictable soundtrack. Unlike many man-made sounds, birdsong is "stochastic"—made up of lots of random notes that cannot be predicted. There are no repeating patterns to focus on and it doesn't get stuck in your head for eternity like the dreaded ear worm. This creates a conscious state where the body relaxes, but the mind is alert. Listening to birdsong is also, of course, an uplifting and transporting experience and, as bird populations decline, one of nature's most precious and valued sounds.

The best way to encourage more birdsong into your garden is, of course, to attract more birds. I have a feeder outside my kitchen window which is a constant food stop for the local sparrows, blue tits, goldfinch, and starlings. Sometimes a wren or a nuthatch also makes an appearance. It's good to know that when they are not noisily tucking into sunflower seeds, these birds could be feeding their young in a nest nearby or singing their songs to each other from the branches of a tree.

CHIMES ON THE WIND

Mostly I prefer nothing but natural sounds in the garden, but there is one exception. The hot tub is tucked away in a little enclosed area planted with a coppice of willow and hazel trees. Among the branches, I have hung two bamboo wind chimes. Each is fitted with metal rods tuned to various notes which strike when moved by the breeze. The sound then resonates beautifully in each bamboo chamber, making a sound a little like a Tibetan bowl. One chime is called *Aqua* (Latin for water), and the other is called *Ignis* (Latin for "fire"). The two sing harmoniousiy together, much like the hot tub which is filled with water and heated by fire. The sound of the wind chimes adds an elemental dimension to the experience of outdoor bathing, turning what could be a simple soak into something more significant.

Although relatively new to Western culture, wind chimes in various forms have existed for thousands of years. Some were intended to have a practical function: farmers in Bali used pieces of bamboo strung up to keep birds off the paddy fields, for example. In ancient Rome, wind bells were believed to keep malevolent spirits at a distance. Metal bells strung outside temples or struck as part of a ceremony have long been used in prayer and meditation.

PLANTS THAT RUSTLE

The swish of the wind as it passes through certain plants or rattles seedheads is a soothing sound on a late summer day. Plant a few of the following plants for maximum effect:

Greater quaker grass (*Briza maxima*): an annual grass whose nodding flowers rustle in the wind.

Love-in-a-mist (*Nigella damascena*): the puffy seedheads of this pretty annual rattle when shaken by a breeze.

Sweetcorn: resist picking every cob and leave a couple of plants. The large, papery leaves rustle pleasingly in the wind. Sweetcorn also relies on wind for dispersal of its pollen.

Bamboo (*Phyllostachys*): the foliage of this large bamboo plant whispers in the wind, while its stems knock together to create a hollow sound. (You can also make wind chimes with the larger canes.)

Banana plant (*Musa*): the huge leaves of the banana sway softly, making gentle shushing sounds.

Eucalyptus: these evergreen plants rustle all year round. Choose a smaller one such as *Eucalyptus archeri*, whose foliage gets louder as it grows, and plant it in a big container by the door so you can hear the wind rifling through it.

Briza

Sweetcorn

The moon garden

How often do you go into the garden at night? Usually we retreat indoors, pulling the drapes tight, locking the door, and turning our backs on what lies outside. What we are also doing is shutting out the most magical time of day. During dusk and just afterward is when the garden is at its most enchanted, yet we can be fearful to venture out to enjoy it even though it is usually quite safe. I've found that when I do leave the sofa and step outside, especially during the full moon, I wonder why I don't do it more often. Moonlight, especially on a still, cloudless night, bathes the garden in silver, picking out white flowers which glow in its rays and causing the pond to shimmer and sparkle. Nocturnal animals start to stir, and if I'm lucky I might see a bat or an owl. The garden is transformed into something bewitching and thrilling.

One way to encourage twilight and post-twilight adventures is to turn a pocket of your outdoor space into a "moon garden." If your garden is big enough, find a spot as far away from neighbors and natural light as possible—you don't want to be troubled by light pollution or noise. Notice how the moon moves across the sky and where and when is the best place to see it. Introduce a seat where you can sit and be still. You might like to add a circular pool, or a flat bowl of water to reflect the moon. Choose plants that come to life at night, either because of their scent or their luminescence.

Try some of these plants:

Night-scented plants: honeysuckle (*Lonicera periclymenum*); jasmine (*Jasminum officinale*); night-scented stock (*Matthiola longipetala*); night-scented phlox (*Zaluzianskya ovata*).

Silver-leaved plants: lavender cotton (*Santolina chamaecyparissus*); honey flower (*Melianthus major*); mugwort (*Artemisia*); daisy bush (*Brachyglottis greyi*); lamb's ear (*Stachys byzantina*).

White foliage and flowers: Shasta daisy (*Leucanthemum* × *superbum*); Queen Anne's lace (*Daucus carota*); Madonna lily (*Lilium candidum*); *Rosa* "Iceberg"; moonflower (*Ipomoae alba*).

Loved by night-time pollinators such as moths: angel's trumpet (*Brugmansia*); jasmine (*Jasminum officinale*); evening primrose (*Oenothera biennis*).

Once you have created your moon garden, go there whenever you can to sit and be quiet. Let your eyes adjust to the light and gaze up at the stars. Let the spirit of your patch of land speak to you and listen to see if you can hear any wild creatures.

The scented garden

It often catches me unawares as I walk along the path doing some other job. My nose twitches. What is that heavenly smell? I lift my head, stop pushing the wheelbarrow, and try to find its source. My nose leads me to the daphne bush which is covered with clusters of pink flowers and humming with bees. I bury my nose among the pretty scented blooms and inhale. The fragrance is so sweet and heady, it is hard to stop breathing deeply. Finally, though, I do, my mundane tasks made easier by the wonderful smell.

A scented garden is like a hidden garden—invisible, often overlooked, but magical. Add fragrance-rich plants to your patch and you add an extra dimension of interest and loveliness. Fragrance elicits emotions and evokes memories like no other sense. It can take us back to another garden or remind us of a particular person. Or it can simply lift the mood for a moment, our spirit raised on a cloud of perfume.

Scented plants have the greatest impact in smaller, contained areas. They are perfect if you have a small city garden or courtyard, for example, where the fragrance circulates and doesn't get carried away on the wind. Plant them where you walk past and where you can reach out and crush a leaf, sniff a bloom, or brush against them to release the aromas. Although flowers are the go-to for the headiest scents, don't ignore aromatic plants like rosemary, which is heady planted as a hedge, or creeping thyme (*Thymus serpyllum*) or Corsican mint (*Mentha requienii*) sown in cracks in paving underfoot. Choose a few favorite scented plants and place them carefully, rather than planting a whole heap of different ones willy-nilly. You want to be able to identify and enjoy each aroma, not have to disentangle many competing ones.

And the best way to enjoy their scent? Rather than inhale deeply, as I cannot resist doing with my daphne, perfume experts recommend taking short sniffs to get the maximum olfactory uplift.

HEAVENLY SCENTS

There are countless scented plants to choose from, and if you plan carefully you can fill the garden with fragrance all year round. Some winter-flowering shrubs are especially heady as they have to work harder to attract the few pollinators around in the colder months.

In the winter

Winter daphne (*Daphne odora*): emits wafts of heavenly fragrance from later winter to early spring.

Mimosa (*Acacia dealbata*): festooned with long clusters of fragrant yellow flowers at the end of winter, this small tree always bucks me up when I most need it. Great in small gardens.

Winter-flowering honeysuckle (*Lonicera fragrantissima*): during the coldest part of the year, this hums with solitary bees attracted by its sublime scent.

Dwarf sweet box (*Sarcococca hookeriana* var. *humilis*): planted near the bird feeder, the sweet fragrance of this unassuming shrub always catches me unawares.

Daphne odora

Honeysuckle

In the spring

Hyacinths (*Hyacinthus*): recently I have planted hyacinth bulbs alongside tulips in pots to provide a heady scent along with cheerful blooms in spring.

Star magnolia (*Magnolia stellata*): this pretty tree pushes its white, star-shaped flowers out before its leaves and releases a lovely perfume as it does so, especially on warmer days.

Apple (*Malus domestica*): I'm really lucky to have an orchard and little gives me as much pleasure as drifting through the trees in spring, inhaling the delicate scent of apple blossom while admiring the beautiful pink and white blooms against a pale blue sky.

Wisteria: every year I watch my wisteria with trepidation. Will it bloom again? Did I prune it at the right time? Has it had enough water? And every year it proves these to be foolish anxieties as its pale purple flowers drape an old fence and fill the air with their delicate scent.

In the summer

Mock orange (*Philadelpus delavayi*): the highly fragrant, pure white flowers of this shrub are one of the scents of summer for me. Smelling a lot like orange blossom, especially on warm summer evenings, this shrub is also adored by bees.

Climbing roses: it's almost impossible not to bury your nose in a rose as you catch a waft of its fragrance. My two favorite roses are "The Generous Gardener", whose musty-scented flowers keep coming all summer, and "Gertrude Jekyll", which flowers early and keeps going for ages.

Lavender (*Lavandula*): one of the most recognizable scents in the garden is also the most soothing. Pick the flowers at their most pungent—midsummer— dry them, then pack them into lavender bags for a fragrant sock drawer or to tuck under a pillow. An essential oil made from its flowers can also help you sleep and generally calm frayed nerves.

Lavender

Scented geraniums (*Pelargonium x hortorum*): it's the leaves, not the flowers, of these plants (which are actually pelargoniums) that are aromatic. So much so that they are classified as herbs and have many uses in aromatherapy and herbal medicine. The smell varies depending on the variety, ranging from apples, apricots, cinnamon, citrus, and lavender. The flowers are pretty and often trail, making them good for window boxes or hanging baskets.

In the fall

Rosemary (*Salvia rosmarinus*): the fat bush of rosemary by my back door is covered with lilac flowers and hums with bees in the spring, but it is good all year round. I love brushing past it in the fall and crushing some of its leaves in my hand.

Pine (*Pinus*): I don't have a pine tree in my garden, unfortunately, but there is a lane nearby which is lined with them. In the fall, fallen pine needles create a soft carpet that releases a fresh smell when trodden upon. I also ferret about looking for pine cones to bring home and heap up in bowls to introduce that distinctive smell, which is so good and clean.

Fragrant gladiolus (*Gladiolus murielae*): plant these bulbs in the spring to be rewarded with pretty white blooms on long stems in late summer/early fall. Their heady scent is a welcome addition to the garden as the days shorten and other flowers fade.

Tobacco plant (*Nicotiana*): there are many varieties of *Nicotiana,* from the tall, stately *N. sylvestris* to the pale-yellow, multiheaded *N. langsdorfii* (my favorite). Not only are the flowers beautiful and long-lasting, producing blooms until the first frost, but they also have a gorgeous, sweet perfume.

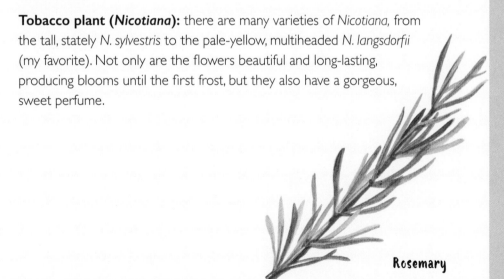

Rosemary

OTHER MAGICAL GARDEN SMELLS

Wood smoke: smoke from a wood fire is, for me, one of the most magical smells there is. When the firepit is lit and starts to crackle, the smell of wood burning draws people close, noses twitching. As the smoke drifts and curls into the air, it brings with it all kinds of associations with the wild, the woods, and other worlds. I love the way it clings to my clothes and how I can still smell it the next day as I pull on the same sweater.

The smell of wood smoke varies depending on what tree is burned. Fruit trees, such as apple, cherry, or pear, have a pleasant, light fragrance, whereas cedar and pine have a stronger, slightly astringent smell. Wood from palo santo (*Bursera graveolens*), a wild tree from South America, when burned is said to clear negative energy, relieve pain, and repel mosquitoes. (*palo santo* means "holy wood.") It can be burned at the start of a ritual or ceremony to clear the space in readiness for magical work. I lit a piece and wafted it around the front and back door of my house when I moved in, to protect those inside and keep us safe.

Forest smells: a walk in the woods in fall releases all manner of wonderful smells as nature begins its tidying up process of decomposition. There is the earthy smell of damp moss and of mushrooms erupting from the ground, then decaying. Fallen leaves pile up underfoot, releasing their smell of decay as they turn into humus.

Petrichor: this is the earthy scent produced by rain falling on very dry ground. It is especially potent during a storm after a period of hot, sunny weather. According to the Met Office in the UK, this sweet, earthy smell is caused by raindrops landing on dusty or clay soils which trap tiny air bubbles on the surface. These then shoot upward before bursting and throwing scent into the air, which is then distributed by the wind. It is a welcome smell for sure, the rain bringing parched gardens back to life.

Cut grass: I am trying my best to reduce the amount of lawn in my garden, letting it grow wild where possible and introducing more wildflowers to attract insects and pollinators. However, I still love the circular patch that remains, especially when it has just been mown. It feels like a carpet beneath my feet and is lovely to walk on barefoot when the dew has settled there in the morning. The scent of the grass as the mower runs over it is also irresistible: the smell of summer in one noseful.

Wind: the air made visible

You can hear, feel, and—sometimes—smell the wind, but you can't see it. Unless it is obstructed in some way, that is. A breeze blowing through a flag brings it to fluttering life. Wind passing through a weather vane causes it to spin. Mobiles hung from trees twist and tinkle when disturbed by a current of air. By introducing elements that play with the wind, we make the element of Air visible and feel its presence in the garden.

READING THE WIND

It can be difficult to understand exactly what the wind is doing. One way to understand it is to put up a weather vane at a high point—on the roof a garage or shed, for example—where it can catch the wind. This will reveal the prevailing direction by pointing directly at the wind, not away from it, and is a good way to understand your local weather patterns. It's worth knowing that if you live in a city, the wind will blow in a different way to the wind that blows across a field of wheat or over a hill. Buildings create obstructions that aren't found in nature and urban winds have lower speeds and higher turbulence, especially at the base of skyscrapers where downdrafts create strong gusts.

An expression of hope: prayer flags

You have probably seen images of Tibetan Buddhist prayer flags fluttering in the wind outside temples or strung across mountain paths in the Himalayas. The purpose of these brightly colored pieces of fabric is not to offer prayers to a god, however. Tibetans believe the wind will blow mantras of goodwill and compassion to everyone in the surrounding area and beyond. This tradition dates back thousands of years and predates Buddhism. The colors used for each flag—blue, white, red, green, and yellow—were originally meant to honor the nature gods of the native Bon religion. Each color represents a different element: blue is space (or Spirit); white is Air; red is Fire; green is Water; and yellow is Earth. They are always strung in this sequence, from left to right.

Over time, Buddhist symbols and mantras were printed over the plain flags. The flags are left unhemmed, so they will eventually fray and disintegrate, symbolizing the inevitable passing of all things. New flags are hung over the old ones, which can be taken down and burned to release the last of the blessings.

MAKE YOUR OWN PRAYER FLAGS

Creating your own prayer flags to hang in the garden is an excellent way of sending messages of hope and compassion, and articulating dreams and wishes, on the wind and out into the world. All you need are pieces of fabric about 5in (12cm) wide and 12in (30cm) long. Try and find some bits of material lying around the house rather than buying new. The number of pieces is up to you. Fold the top of each piece down (about 3in (8cm) should do it) and stitch into place to allow a piece of string or cord to run through it easily. Don't hem the flag: you want it fade, fray, and fall apart over time.

Think of what your intention for each flag is. It could be to help someone going through a difficult time, or it could be a long-held dream you want to realize, or it could be a wider, more general wish such as an end to human conflict. Or it could be something quite different.

Decorate the flags with fabric paint, embroidery, or simply by drawing on them with a Sharpie. String the flags up on a piece of string or cord and hang somewhere where the breeze will catch them and spread your good wishes far and wide.

Wind sculptures and spinners

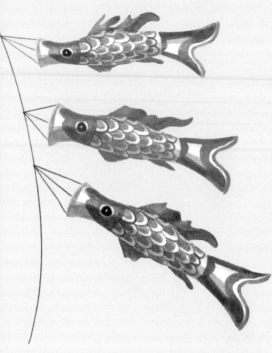

Anyone who has ever been to a festival will have seen various wind-catching devices popping up around the tents and performance spaces. They bring a colorful festival vibe to the proceedings (and are also a handy way to locate your tent!) as they move in the summer breeze.

My favorite is the classic windsock, a tube mounted on a pole, which indicates the direction and strength of the wind. Most of these are intended as measuring devices, especially useful at airports, but there are also more colorful ones shaped like Japanese carp. These *koinobori*, or carp streamers, are traditionally flown in Japan to celebrate Children's Day. They are often hung in groups so that it looks like a shoal of carp flying through the sky.

One of these wouldn't really suit my rural Herefordshire garden, however, so I looked at wind sculptures and spinners instead. These kinetic objects (objects with moving parts) change shape and direction as the wind passes through them. Many artists have created incredible wind sculptures that move hypnotically in the wind, sometimes completely changing their shape and appearance. They are feats of engineering as much as works of art and well worth looking out for in public spaces.

Fortunately, smaller ones exist for private gardens. I put mine in the orchard where the wind catches it, to connect with the element of Air. It is a beautiful, ever-changing decoration that draws the eye, and the feet, toward it.

An air ritual

The simplest and most powerful way to connect with the element of Air is to become more aware of your breath. Meditation using breath as its focus is common in many different faiths and belief systems. In Buddhist practice, the "mindfulness of breathing" technique uses the breath to aid concentration and bring meditators back to the present moment, rather than letting the mind drift. Similarly, the Sanskrit word *pranayama* is the yogic practice of focusing on the breath. (*Prana* means "vital life force" and *yama* means "to gain control.")

For the modern witch, breathing exercises and meditation with breathwork can help prepare your body and mind for magic work, and bring you back down to earth afterward. Some people also use their breath to send energies and good wishes to other people (see ritual overleaf)

THE BREATH OF JOY

This yoga exercise is my favorite way to start the day. It only takes a few minutes, but its effects are long lasting. I always feel re-energized and uplifted. When the weather is warm enough (and not raining heavily!), I do it outside in the middle of the circular lawn where I can take fresh air into my lungs, look at the faraway hills, and listen to birdsong.

Before you begin the exercise, and if you have time, it's beneficial to take a few moments to "arrive" and release any tension that you may be holding in your mind or body. Sit in a comfortable position with your hands in your lap. Keep the back of your neck long and lengthen your spine. Sink into the position and let your face, mouth, and jaws soften. Pay attention to your breathing and be aware of air inflating your lungs, and then exiting and deflating. Visualize the air spreading throughout your body into every cell. Continue with this awareness of breath for a few minutes and then, when you are ready, get up on your feet. Now you are in a good mental and physical state to do the breath of joy.

Stand with both feet firmly planted on the ground, a hip-width apart. Do it barefoot to feel really rooted to the earth.

Stage one Take one deep breath in, then one long breath out. Let the air fill the lowest part of the lungs and, as it does so, swing your arms in front of you with the palms facing upward.

Stage two

Take another deep breath in, and another long breath out. This time, let the air fill the middle part of the lungs and, as it does so, open your arms to the side, keeping the palms facing upward.

Stage three

Take a third deep breath in, and another long breath out. Let the air fill the top part of your lungs and, as it does so, lift your arms up to the sky with your palms facing each other.

End by exhaling completely and diving forward with your arms reaching behind you like a bird diving toward the earth.

Repeat the three stages nine times.

Once you have finished the exercise, sit down and close your eyes. Place your hands on your lower belly and direct your breath toward them. Take a few slow breaths and start to "re-enter" your body, feeling its contact with the ground and becoming aware of the sights and sounds around you. Gently move your hands and feet and open your eyes. Observe how you feel. Hopefully, you will feel joyful and lively and ready to start the day.

Resources

BOOKS

Avalon, Annwyn, *Water Witchcraft: Magic and Lore from the Celtic Tradition* (Red Wheel, 2019).

Bowes, Susan, *Notions and Potions: A Safe, Practical Guide to Creating Magic and Miracles* (Sterling Publishing, 1997).

Chamberlain, Lisa, *Wicca Elemental Magic* (Chamberlain Publications, 2014).

Culpeper, Nicholas, *Complete Herbal* (Various editions; first published 1652).

Cunningham, Scott, *Cunningham's Encyclopedia of Magical Herbs* (Llewellyn Publications, 2020).

Guiley, Rosemary Ellen, *The Encyclopedia of Witches and Witchcraft* (Facts on File Limited, 1989).

Pullen, Mandy and Embleton, Jane, *Sun, Moon and Clock* (Mapless Publishing, 2022).

Reynolds, Mary, *The Garden Awakening: Designs to Nurture Our Land and Ourselves* (Green Books, 2016).

ORGANIZATIONS

American Society of Dowsers, dowsers.org

British Society of Dowsers, britishdowsers.org

Charles Dowding (No Dig), charlesdowding.org

Findhorn Foundation, findhorn.org

Garden Organic, gardenorganic.org.uk

The Order of Bards Druids and Ovates, druidry.org.

The Soil Association, soilassociation.org

Index